BARCLAYS stage

TRAVERSE
THEATRE

**Traverse Theatre,
Cambridge Arts Theatre and
The Oxford Playhouse present the
Traverse Theatre Company's production of**

WIDOWS

by Ariel Dorfman
in collaboration with Tony Kushner

.

EUROPEAN PREMIERE

First performed at the Cambridge Arts Theatre
Wednesday 5 March 1997

Partners *with* THE ARTS COUNCIL OF ENGLAND

Cambridge Arts
Theatre

THE OXFORD
PLAYHOUSE

KT-170-767

ARIEL DORFMAN is a Chilean expatriate who has made a second home for himself in the United States. He is a Distinguished Professor at Duke University, North Carolina, where he lives with his wife, Angelica, and their youngest son Joaquin.

Dorfman is well known for his cultural criticism and has also written five novels, including the recent *Konfidenz*, a collection of short stories and a book of poems. His plays include *Reader* (first produced by the Traverse in 1995) and the much acclaimed *Death and the Maiden*, which won the Olivier Award for Best Play and was adapted for film by the author and directed by Roman Polanski. With his eldest son, Rodrigo, he recently wrote the BBC teleplay, *Prisoners In Time*, starring John Hurt, which won the Writers Guild Award as *Best Screenplay of the Year*. He has been called the "*conscience of the New World Order*" (Washington Post) and "*a story-teller of almost mythic proportions*" (Financial Times).

TONY KUSHNER is the author of the celebrated *Angels in America*, which has won innumerable theatre awards and is being adapted for film by Robert Altman. Kushner has also written *A Bright Room Called Day*, *Slavs!* and *The Illusion* (adapted from *Corneille*). He lives in New York.

TRAVERSE THEATRE

Over the last three decades Edinburgh's Traverse Theatre has had a seminal influence on British and international theatre. With quality, award-winning productions and programming, the Traverse receives accolades at home and abroad from audiences and critics alike.

Traverse productions have been seen world-wide. Most recently, BONDAGERS toured the world, delighting audiences in Edinburgh, London, Toronto and Budapest. After sell-out Edinburgh runs MOSCOW STATIONS transferred to both the West End and to New York; UNIDENTIFIED HUMAN REMAINS transferred to London's Hampstead Theatre; and after touring the Highlands and Islands of Scotland KNIVES IN HENS transferred to a sell-out season at the Bush Theatre in London. No stranger to awards, the Traverse recently won the *Scotland on Sunday Critics Award* for SHINING SOULS by Chris Hannan.

As Scotland's new writing theatre, the Traverse is a powerhouse of quality experimentation, artistic diversity and the place to see some of the most important contemporary theatre work around. The Theatre commissions the best new writers from Scotland and around the world; facilitates numerous script development workshops, rehearsed readings and public writing workshops; and aims to produce six major new theatre productions plus a Scottish touring production each year.

An essential element of the Traverse Company's activities takes place within the educational sector, concentrating on the process of new writing in schools. The Traverse is unique in its exclusive dedication to new writing, providing the infrastructure, professional support and expertise to ensure the development of a sustainable and relevant theatre culture for Scotland and the UK.

WIDOWS

by Ariel Dorfman
in collaboration with Tony Kushner

Director	Ian Brown
Designer	Mark Leese
Lighting Designer	Howard Harrison
Composer	John Irvine
Movement Director	Caroline Salem
Assistant Director	John Tiffany

Alexis	Billy Boyd
Narrator/Alonso	Colin Gourley
Fidelia	Molly Innes
Rosa/Beatrice Kastoria	Anne Kidd
Yanina	Pauline Knowles
Sofia Fuentes	Edith Maccarthur
Alexandra Fuentes	Irene Macdougall
Emmanuel	Neil McKinven
Katherina	Hilary Maclean
Lieutenant	Michael Nardone
Doctor/Father Gabriel/ *Philip Kastoria* }	John Ramage
Teresa Salas	Ann-Louise Ross
Captain	Sean Scanlan
Cecilia Sanjines	Anne Marie Timoney

all other parts played by members of the company

Company Stage Manager	Gavin Johnston
Deputy Stage Manager	Kay Courteney-Chrystal
Assistant Stage Manager	Victoria Paulo
Wardrobe Supervisor	Anna Lau
Wardrobe Assistant	Alice Taylor

BILLY BOYD *(Alexis)*: Tained: RSAMD. Theatre work includes: SLEEPING BEAUTY, THE MERCHANT OF VENICE, MERLIN THE MAGNIFICENT (Royal Lyceum); THE PLAZA (Tron showcase); TRAINSPOTTING (G& J UK Tour); MUCH ADO ABOUT NOTHING (Cottier/Original Shakespeare Co.); THE SLAB BOYS, THE SECRET DIARY OF ADRIAN MOLE (Byre); THE WEAVERS, THE THREEPENNY OPERA (New Atheneum); AGAMEMNON (Warsaw Academy); TO THE LAST LETTER (Stirling Heritage Co.). Television includes: TAGGART, JULIE AND THE CADILLACS.

IAN BROWN *(Director)*: Ian was Artistic Director of the Traverse Theatre from 1988-1996. Productions for the Traverse include: SHINING SOULS *by Chris Hannan*, BONDAGERS *by Sue Glover*, STONES AND ASHES *by Daniel Danis*, READER *by Ariel Dorfman*, THE COLLECTION *by Mike Cullen*, AWAY *by Michael Gow*, UNIDENTIFIED HUMAN REMAINS AND THE TRUE NATURE OF LOVE, POOR SUPER MAN *by Brad Fraser* (Traverse/Hampstead), TRAINSPOTTING *adapted by Harry Gibson* (Citizens'), TALLY'S BLOOD *by Ann-Marie di Mambro*, THE HOPE SLIDE *by Joan McLeod*, INES DE CASTRO, A LIGHT IN THE VILLAGE *by John Clifford* (Traverse and BBC TV), MOSCOW STATIONS *adapted by Stephen Mulrine* (Traverse, Garrick & Union Square, N.Y.), ANNA - AN OPERA *by John Clifford and Craig Armstrong*, BUCHANAN *by Tom McGrath*, LOOSE ENDS *by Stuart Hepburn*, THE HOUSE AMONG THE STARS *by Michel Tremblay*, COLUMBUS *by Michele Celeste*, PIGPLAY *by Raymond Cousse*, THE BENCH *by Alexander Gelman*, THE COW JUMPED OVER THE MOON *by Donna Franceschild* and HARDIE AND BAIRD *by James Kelman*. Ian was formerly Artistic Director of TAG Theatre Company and before that Associate Director of the Theatre Royal Stratford East. In September 1996 he directed *Sam Shepard's* FOOL FOR LOVE at the Donmar Warehouse and directed Clyde Unity's adaptation of *Armistead Maupin's* BABYCAKES in Spring 1997.

COLIN GOURLEY *(Narrator/Alonso)*: Trained: RSAMD. Theatre work includes: THE IMPORTANCE OF BEING EARNEST (Royal Lyceum); MAJOR BARBARA, WUTHERING HEIGHTS, THE KITCHEN, GOOD, PRAVDA, ALL MY SONS, NOISES OFF (Perth); WOMAN IN MIND, DAPHNE LAUREOLA, SEE HOW THEY RUN (Pitlochry Festival Theatre); MACBETH, MR GILLIE, LIFE OF GALILEO, JAMIE THE SAXT (Scottish Theatre Co.); ANE SATIRE OF THE THRIE ESTAITES, A WEE TOUCH OF CLASS (Edinburgh Festival); ROBIN HOOD, UNLAWFUL KILLING (Theatre Royal, Stratford East); THE LATE CHRISTOPHER BEAN, HOW THE OTHER HALF LOVES (Cambridge Theatre Co.); ON THE RAZZLE, THE THREE MUSKETEERS (Nuffield, Southampton); A CHRISTMAS CAROL (English Theatre Co., Stockholm); DOUBLE DOUBLE (Frankfurt); THE CHAMPION OF PARIBANOU, HARD TIMES, GRIMM TALES (Stephen Joseph Theatre in the Round). Television includes: THE BILL, TAGGART, EASTENDERS, THE MAN FROM AUNTIE, THEIFTAKERS. Many radio broadcasts including: WHAT EVERY WOMAN KNOWS (BBC World Service); PEGGERS AND CREELERS (BBC Radio 4); MORNING STORY.

HOWARD HARRISON *(Lighting Designer)*: Trained: Central School Of Speech And Drama. Theatre work includes: GREEK, DECADENCE, MATADOR, 900 ONEONTA, AIN'T MISBEHAVIN', THE DUCHESS OF SYLVIA and OLD WICKED SONGS (all West End); LITTLE SHOP OF HORRORS (Singapore Repertory Theatre); MACBETH (Crucible, Sheffield); NIGHT MUST FALL (Windsor/Bromley); JUST SO (Tricycle); EAST LYNNE, NORTHANGER ABBEY, HUCKLEBERRY FINN (Greenwich Theatre); OTHELLO, THEY SHOOT HORSES DON'T THEY? (National Youth Theatre); LOOT (Churchill Bromley/West Yorkshire Playhouse); THE FLIGHT INTO EGYPT (Hampstead); FOOL FOR LOVE (Donmar Warehouse); LORD OF THE FLIES, HENRY VIII (Royal Shakespeare Company); ROSENCRANTZ AND GUILDENSTERN ARE DEAD, BLUE REMEMBERED HILLS (Royal National Theatre). Opera includes: AIDA (Royal Opera House); BEATRICE AND BENEDICT, CAVALLERIA RUSTICANA/PAGLIACCI (Welsh National Opera); THE BARBER OF SEVILLE (Austalian Opera); THE MAKROPULOS CASE (Metropolitan Opera, New York).

MOLLY INNES *(Fidelia)*: Theatre work includes: SHINING SOULS, STONES AND ASHES, (Traverse); CROSS DRESSING IN THE DEPRESSION (Peter Mackie Burns); DREAMING IN PUBLIC (Traverse & Byre); DOING BIRD (Cat A Theatre Co.); PLAYBOY OF THE WESTERN WORLD (Communicado); THE STRANGE CASE OF DR JEKYLL AND MR HYDE, TO KILL A MOCKING BIRD, THE PRIME OF MISS JEAN BRODIE (Royal Lyceum); STINGING SEA (Citizens'); TARTUFFE (Dundee Rep); GLORIA GOODHEART AND THE GLITTER GRAB GANG, JOLLY ROBERT AND THE PIRATES FROM SPACE (Theatre Workshop); MURDER AND THE MUSIC HALL (Theatre Public). Television includes: THE BILL, A MUGS GAME; TAKIN' OVER THE ASYLUM; THE FERGUSON THEORY; STRATHBLAIR; RAB C. NESBITT. Radio includes: BILL 'N' KOO, SOME OF MY BEST FRIENDS ARE DOLPHINS (BBC Radio 4), THE FOURTH FOREIGNER. Film: STELLA DOES TRICKS.

JOHN IRVINE *(Composer)*: Trained: RSAMD, University of Edinburgh. Theatre work includes: MOSCOW STATIONS (Traverse, Garrick & Union Square, N.Y.), POOR SUPERMAN, UNIDENTIFIED HUMAN REMAINS (Traverse & Hampstead), SHINING SOULS, STONES AND ASHES, READER, EUROPE, THE HOPE SLIDE, BROTHERS OF THUNDER, BUCHANAN, THE LIFE OF STUFF, COLUMBUS: BLOODING THE OCEAN, THE STRUGGLE OF THE DOGS AND THE BLACK (Traverse); TRAINSPOTTING (Citizens' & Bush); THE STRANGE CASE OF DR JEKYLL AND MR HYDE (Lyceum); THE NEW MENOZA (Gate); QUIET NIGHT IN (KTC, Tramway); WHITE BIRD PASSES (Dundee Rep); SEVEN-TENTHS (Walk The Plank); PINNOCHIO (Visible Fictions). Film includes: DOG DAYS (NFTS).

ANNE KIDD (*Rosa/Beatrice Kastoria*): Theatre work includes: BORN GUILTY (7:84); THE GRAPES OF WRATH (7:84/Dundee Rep); THE SNOW QUEEN (MacRobert Arts Centre); SCOTS QUAIR (TAG); THE PRICE (Royal Lyceum); SPIDER'S WEB, THE NORMAN CONQUESTS (Pitlochry Festival Theatre); THE DEEP BLUE SEA, MY COUSIN RACHEL, ONE FLEW OVER THE CUCKOO'S NEST (Perth Rep); THE RISING OF THE MOON (Old Red Lion); RELATIVELY SPEAKING (Watermill); AGNES OF GOD (Belgrade Studio, Coventry); DUET FOR ONE (Birmingham Rep); MOTHER COURAGE, THE MATCHMAKER, BRAND, LOVE'S LABOURS LOST (Nottingham Playhouse); ANDROCLES AND THE LION (Regent's Park Open Air); WHAT EVERY WOMAN KNOWS (Brunton); OLD TIMES (Exeter). Television includes: DOCTOR FINLAY, TAGGART (STV); TUTTI FRUTTI, THE LOVE SCHOOL, THE GHOST SONATA, SUTHERLAND'S LAW, ANGLES, DOCTOR FINLAY'S CASEBOOK, KING ARTHUR (BBC). Film includes: PORT OF SECRETS.

PAULINE KNOWLES (*Yanina*): Theatre work includes: THE COLLECTION, MARISOL (Traverse); KNIVES IN HENS (Traverse & Bush, London); MEN SHOULD WEEP, SCOTS QUAIR (TAG); SWING HAMMER SWING (Citizens'); ELEGIES FOR ANGELS, PUNKS AND RAGING QUEENS (Luckenbooth); TWELFTH NIGHT (Royal Lyceum & Salisbury Theatre); CUTTIN' A RUG, SCHOOL FOR WIVES (Royal Lyceum); ANTIGONE, JUMP THE LIFE TO COME (7:84); OH WHAT A LOVELY WAR, SHARKS, CLEANING UP (Wildcat); VODKA AND DAISIES (Annexe); DON JUAN (Penname); ALADDIN (Skint Knees). Television includes: ACTING-WITH RICHARD WILSON, STRATHBLAIR, JOHN BROWN'S BODY. Radio includes: FLOATING, SUBUTU PASSAGE, WANTIN' A HAND, LEAVE ME ALONE.

MARK LEESE (*Designer*): For the Traverse: FAITH HEALER, THE HOPE SLIDE, BROTHERS OF THUNDER, KNIVES IN HENS (also Bush); PARALLEL LINES (Theatre Cryptic); FROGS (Royal National Theatre); BRILLIANT TRACES (Diva/Tron); BABES IN THE WOOD, SNOW WHITE, LOVE & LIBERTY (Tron); BORN GUILTY, THE WAR IN HEAVEN, THE GRAPES OF WRATH, THE SALT WOUND, ANTIGONE (7:84); ON GOLDEN POND (Lyceum); BLACK COMEDY, PUBLIC EYE (Watford Palace). Film includes: CALIFORNIA SUNSHINE (Sigma Films); GOOD DAY FOR THE BAD GUYS (Greenbridge Films); WHAT ELEPHANTS (WWF).

EDITH MACARTHUR *(Sofia Fuentes)*: Many theatre credits include: THE FLOURES O' EDINBURGH, ON GOLDEN POND, LONG DAY'S JOURNEY INTO NIGHT, THE CHERRY ORCHARD, THE CIRCLE, SEPARATE TABLES, ARSENIC AND OLD LACE, PYGMALION, PRIDE AND PREJUDICE, DAPHNE LAUREOLA (Pitlochry Festival Theatre); DRIVING MISS DAISY, WHAT EVERY WOMAN KNOWS (Perth Rep); GOOD (Tron); HAY FEVER, CHARLEY'S AUNT, DEATH OF A SALESMAN (Royal Lyceum); CINDERELLA (King's, Edinburgh); JAMIE THE SAXT, THE WALLACE (Scottish Theatre Co.); ANE SATYRE OF THE THRIE ESTAITES (Edinburgh Festival and Warsaw International Festival); THE LION IN WINTER, RELATIVELY SPEAKING, GHOSTS, THE CHERRY ORCHARD (Theatre Season, Octertyre Castle, Creiff); THE PRIME OF MISS JEAN BRODIE (London's West End 1997 & 1994/5). Television includes: HIGH ROAD, THE BORDERERS, SUNSET SONG, WEIR OF HERMISTON, SUTHERLAND'S LAW, ROB ROY, THE SANDBAGGERS, FRENCH FIELDS, LA FORGA DE UN REBELDE, MENACE UNSEEN, GENERAL HOSPITAL, CONSEQUENCES, THE MELODY LINGERS ON. Radio includes: BETTER TO BREAK YOUR NECK, FLOATING, MISS WILMOTT'S GHOST, NAPOLEON, I - KANDINSKY.

IRENE MACDOUGALL *(Alexandra Fuentes)*: Theatre work includes: UNIDENTIFIED HUMAN REMAINS (Traverse & Hampstead); THE STRUGGLE OF THE DOGS AND THE BLACK, LOSING VENICE (Traverse). OLD TIMES, MERLIN, THE CRUCIBLE, THE MARRIAGE OF FIGARO, FITTING FOR LADIES, TWELFTH NIGHT, ARMS AND THE MAN, WOYZECK, HAMLET (Royal Lyceum); MUCH ADO ABOUT NOTHING (Ordinary Shakespeare Co.); A MAN WITH CONNECTIONS (Perth Rep & Russia); DRACULA, THE HYPOCONRIAK (Dundee); PRESENT LAUGHTER, ON GOLDEN POND (Pitlochry Festival Theatre). Television includes: DR FINLAY, THE BALDY MAN, FINNEY, RAB C. NESBITT, VANITY FAIR.

NEIL MCKINVEN *(Emmanuel)*: Trained: RADA. Theatre work includes: THE SHIP (Glasgow Docks); ROAD (7:84/Citizens'); UNDERWATER SWIMMING (New End); WHEN I WAS A GIRL I USED TO SCREAM AND SHOUT (National Tour); THE MARK (Cockpit); BABES IN THE WOOD, DAVE'S LAST LAUGH (Tron); AFTERS (Edinburgh Festival). Television includes: TAKIN' OVER THE ASYLUM, STRATHBLAIR, THE SHIP, TAGGART, DEGREES OF ERROR, THE VET.

HILARY MACLEAN *(Katherina)*: Trained: RSAMD. Theatre work includes: PRICKLY HEAT, JUST FRANK, BLENDING IN, GREAT EXPECTATIONS, BONDAGERS (Traverse); THE CONQUEST OF THE SOUTH POLE (Traverse/Royal Court); INES DE CASTRO (Traverse/Riverside); THE MILL ON THE FLOSS (Contact, Manchester); LES LIAISONS DANGEREUSES (Dundee Rep); BOYS STUFF (Sheffield Crucible); GRAVE PLOTS (Nottingham Playhouse); THE SLAB BOYS (Old Red Lion); THE IMPORTANCE OF BEING EARNEST (Royal Lyceum); THE BABY (Tron). Television includes: DOCTOR FINLAY, STRATHBLAIR, TAGGART, THE BILL, WILDERNESS EDGE, INES DE CASTRO. Film includes: BLUE BLACK PERMANENT. Radio includes several plays with BBC Radio Scotland and more recently with BBC Pebble Mill.

MICHAEL NARDONE *(Lieutenant)*: Trained: Queen Margaret College, Edinburgh. Theatre work includes: KNIVES IN HENS, BUCHANAN, EUROPE, MARISOL, THE COLLECTION (Traverse); WILDMAN, SHINDA THE MAGIC APE, THE MARRIAGE OF FIGARO, MERLIN (parts 1 & 2), MIRANDOLINA (Royal Lyceum); SPLATTER (7:84); BOUNCERS, CAIN AND ABEL (Chester Gateway); ELIDOR, TOM SAWYER (Contact, Manchester); THE LEGEND OF ST JULIAN, CYRANO DE BERGERAC, TALES OF THE ARABIAN NIGHTS (Communicado); WHAT EVERY WOMAN KNOWS (Newbury); THE SATIRE OF THE FOURTH ESTATE (Edinburgh Festival). Television includes: DOCTOR FINLAY, TAGGART, HIGH ROAD, MAY AND JUNE. Film includes: CONQUEST, SOFT TOP HARD SHOULDER, BEING HUMAN, I WANT TO BE LIKE YOU.

JOHN RAMAGE *(Doctor/Father Gabriel/Philip Kastoria)*: Theatre work includes: SHINING SOULS, YOUR TURN TO CLEAN THE STAIRS (Traverse); ELEGIES FOR ANGELS, PUNKS AND RAGING QUEENS (Luckenbooth); THE BOYFRIEND, ROUGH CROSSING, H.M.S. PINAFORE, THE MIKADO (Perth Theatre); NIGHT SKY (Stellar Quines); SALVATION (Tron). Numerous tours as well as fifteen pantomime seasons at King's Theatres (Edinburgh and Glasgow), Sunderland Empire, Tron, Royal Lyceum and Perth. He also directed THE LAST OF THE LAIRDS (Perth Theatre) and is a lecturer in Acting Studies at Edinburgh's Queen Margaret College where he has directed over thirty productions. Television includes: THE HIGH LIFE, RAB C. NESBITT. BBC Radio Drama includes: THE SHROUD, POTTED HISTORY.

ANN-LOUISE ROSS (*Teresa Salas*): Theatre work includes: BONDAGERS, BUCHANAN (Traverse); THE NUTCRACKER SUITE, THE HYPOCHONDRIAK, AS YOU LIKE IT, LE BOURGEOIS GENTILHOMME, MEASURE FOR MEASURE, VOLPONE, OTHELLO, DANCING AT LUGHNASA, OUR COUNTRY'S GOOD, THE CAUCASIAN CHALK CIRCLE, HAMLET, THE STEAMIE (Royal Lyceum); THE MARRIAGE OF FIGARO (Royal Lyceum/King's, Glasgow); WHO'S AFRAID OF VIRGINIA WOOLF (Dundee Rep); THE GUID SISTERS (Tron Theatre); KEPLER, NANCY SLEEKIT (Fifth Estate); CIVILIANS / ANIMAL (Scottish Theatre Co); NAE PROBLEM (7:84); ANE SATYRE OF THE THRIE ESTAITES (Edinburgh Festival); CRYING WOLF, A PLACE WITH THE PIGS (Communicado).   Film & Television includes: TRAINSPOTTING, DEAD SEA REELS, TAGGART, PLAY ME SOMETHING, SILENT SCREAM, TICKETS FOR THE ZOO, THE BALL ON THE SLATES, AN ACTORS LIFE FOR ME, HIGH ROAD, CRIME STORY, THE NEGOTIATOR, CRIME LIMITED, THE NEAR ROOM, THE BILL, HAMISH MACBETH.   Radio includes numerous BBC Scotland Schools and Drama programmes.

CAROLINE SALEM (*Movement Director*): Theatre work includes: A MIDSUMMER NIGHT'S DREAM, THE TEMPEST (Salisbury Playhouse); STATES OF SHOCK (Salisbury Playhouse/National Theatre); A MIDSUMMER NIGHT'S DREAM (Open Air Theatre Regents Park); BLUE REMEMBERED HILLS, THE MERCHANT OF VENICE (Crucible Theatre Sheffield).   Work for the Traverse includes: collaborative workshops, STONES AND ASHES and SHINING SOULS.

SEAN SCANLAN (*Captain*): Theatre work includes: NOT WAVING (Traverse); SHAKEN NOT STIRRED (Theatre Royal, Northampton); VIVAT VIVAT REGINA (Mermaid); THE GLASS MENAGERIE, LOVE FOR LOVE, TIMON OF ATHENS, TROILUS AND CRESSIDA, GUYS AND DOLLS, THE COMEDIANS (Bristol Old Vic); PRATTS FALL, CLYDE NOVEAU (Tron); THE ALCHEMIST, THE CHANGELING, (Crucible, Sheffield); HEDDA GABLER (Haymarket, Leicester); AS YOU LIKE IT (Royal Lyceum); PYGMIES IN THE RUINS (Lyric, Belfast); THE LIFE OF STUFF (Donmar Warehouse).   Television work includes: RAB C. NESBITT, HAMISH MACBETH, BERGERAC, PARA HANDY, TAGGART, SENSE OF FREEDOM, CASUALTY, THE BLUES, LEAVING, TUMBLEDOWN, THE BEIDERBECK CONNECTION, CARROT CONFIDENTIAL, ALBERT AND THE LION, THE NEW LEASE OF DEATH (BBC); EBBTIDE, HEARTBEAT, CALL RED, ELLINGTON, CORONATION STREET, SHERLOCK HOLMES, HIGH ROAD, BOON (ITV).   Film work includes: THE BIG MAN, PHANTOM OF THE OPERA, BLUE BLACK PERMANENT, PRISONER OF HONOR, KIM.

JOHN TIFFANY *(Assistant Director)*: Trained: Glasgow University. Assistant Director at the Traverse since August 1995. He has directed PASSING PLACES and SHARP SHORTS, co-directed STONES AND ASHES and was assistant director on SHINING SOULS and THE ARCHITECT for the Traverse. Other work includes: THE SUNSET SHIP (Young Vic); GRIMM TALES (Leicester Haymarket). He set up LOOKOUT, a new writing theatre company in Glasgow, for whom his directing work includes HIDE AND SEEK and BABY, EAT UP. In Spring 1997 he will direct a *Tartan Short*, Kate Atkinson's KARMIC MOTHERS.

ANNE MARIE TIMONEY *(Cecilia Sanjines)*: Trained: RSAMD. Theatre work includes: STONES AND ASHES (Traverse); ASYLUM, ASYLUM, HUGHIE ON THE WIRES (Wiseguise); ONE, TWO, HEY (Arches & touring); HUGHIE ON THE WIRES (Calypso, Dublin); PRE PARADISE SORRY NOW, THE HOUSEKEEPER, ANTHONY, WITTGENSTEIN'S DAUGHTER (Citizens'); CONQUEST OF THE SOUTH POLE, ONE FLEW OVER THE CUCKOO'S NEST (Rain Dog); THE WICKED LADIES (Old Atheneum, Women 2000); MARLENE - FALLING IN LOVE AGAIN (A.B.C. Theatre Co.); OTHELLO, DEATH OF A SALESMAN, THE MERCHANT OF VENICE (Royal Lyceum); ROAD, LONG STORY SHORT (7:84); MARLENE (A.B.C.). Television includes: TAGGART, CRIME FILE, HIGH ROAD, DR FINLAY (STV); THE LONG ROADS, RAB C. NESBITT, RUFFIAN HEARTS, EX-S, BAD BOYS, ATHLETICO PARTICK (BBC). Radio includes: STAND UP NORMA JEAN (BBC). Film work includes: CARLA'S SONG, RIFF RAFF, A CHILL, WILD FLOWERS, SNAKE WOMAN.

The UK tour of WIDOWS is supported by Barclay's Stage Partners in collaboration with the Arts Council of England

WIDOWS props, costumes & scenery built by Traverse workshops.
Funded by the National Lottery

For generous help with WIDOWS the Traverse Theatre thanks:
Rachel George - Scenic Artist
Franziska Metzeger and Alan Glasgow
- production placements
Andrew Meldrum - administration placement
Print Photography by Euan Myles
LEVER BROTHERS for Wardrobe Care

TRAVERSE THEATRE • THE COMPANY

Usha Bagga
Development Asst

Morag Ballantyne
Marketing Mgr

Claire Beattie
Education Co-ordinator

Maria Bechaalani
Asst Electrician

Vian Curtis
Production Technician

Kay Courteney-Chrystal
Deputy Stage Mgr

Emma Dall
Finance Assistant

Rachel Davidson
Deputy Bar Mgr

Lynn Ferguson
Wardrobe Supervisor

Tim Follett
Deputy Electrician

Mike Griffiths
Production Mgr

Paul Hackett
Finance Mgr

Charlotte Halliday
Asst. Marketing Mgr

Noelle Henderson
Development Mgr

Philip Howard
Artistic Director

Louise Ironside
Script Associate

Ruth Kent
Box Office Assistant

Gavin Johnston
Stage Mgr

Niall Macdonald
Bar Mgr

Torquil MacLeod
Front of House Mgr

Jan McTaggart
Marketing Asst

Jenny Mainland
Administrative Asst

Colin Marr
Theatre/Commercial Mgr

Lucy Mason
Administrative Producer

Alex Musgrave
Box Office Mgr

Duncan Nicoll
Asst Bar Mgr

Victoria Paulo
Asst Stage Mgr

Renny Robertson
Chief Electrician

Kirstie Skinner
Asst Administrator

John Tiffany
Asst Director

Jolyon White
Asst Box Office Mgr

Ella Wildridge
Dramaturg

TRAVERSE THEATRE - BOARD OF DIRECTORS

Tom Mitchell; President, **John Scott Moncrieff**; Chair,
Harry McCann; Vice Chair, **Scott Howard**; Secretary,
**Barry Ayre, Paul Chima, Stuart Hepburn,
Sir Eddie Kulukundis, Muriel Murray**

TRAVERSE THEATRE • SPONSORSHIP

Sponsorship income enables the Traverse to commission and produce new plays and offer audiences a diverse and exciting programme of events throughout the year.

We would like to thank the following companies for their support throughout the year.

BANK OF SCOTLAND
A FRIEND FOR LIFE

 E·S·P·C

CORPORATE ASSOCIATE SCHEME

LEVEL ONE
Dundas & Wilson CS
Scottish Brewers
Scottish Life Assurance Co
United Distillers

LEVEL TWO
Allingham & Co, Solicitors
Isle of Skye 8 Year Blend
Laurence Smith - Wine Merchants
NB Information
Mactaggart and Mickel Ltd
Métier Recruitment
The Royal Bank of Scotland
Willis Corroon Scotland Ltd

LEVEL THREE
Alistir Tait FGA Antique & Fine Jewellery, Gerrard & Medd, Designers,
KPMG, Moores Rowland Chartered Accountants,
Nicholas Groves Raines Architects,
Scottish Post Office Board

With thanks to:
Navy Blue Design, designers for the Traverse
and to George Stewarts the printers.
Robin Arnott of the Royal Bank of Scotland for his advise on information technology and systems.
This placement was arranged through Business In The Arts.

The Traverse Theatre's work would not be possible without the support of:

THE SCOTTISH ARTS COUNCIL

·EDINBVRGH·
THE CITY OF EDINBURGH COUNCIL

The Traverse receives financial assistance for its educational and development work from:
Calouste Gulbenkian Foundation,
Esmee Fairbairn Charitable Trust,
The Peggy Ramsay Foundation,
The Nancie Massey Charitable Trust

Charity No.SC 002368

WIDOWS

by Ariel Dorfman with Tony Kushner
adapted from the novel by Ariel Dorfman

2

Cast

The Fuentes Family

SOFIA FUENTES, *the Grandmother*
ALEXANDRA, *married to her son Emiliano*
YANINA, *married to her son Alonso*
FIDELIA, *daughter of Alexandra*
ALEXIS, *son of Alexandra*
ALONSO, *son of Sofia*

The Women of the Valley

TERESA SALAS
KATHERINA
ROSA
MARILUZ
AMANDA
LUCIA
RAMONA

CECILIA SANJINES, *girlfriend of Emmanuel, the Orderly*

PHILIP KASTORIA
BEATRICE KASTORIA, *his wife*
KASTORIA'S BROTHER

FATHER GABRIEL, *the parish priest*

The Army

THE CAPTAIN
THE LIEUTENANT
EMMANUEL, *the orderly*
THE DOCTOR
SOLDIERS

THE NARRATOR

There can be fewer valley women, and there can be many more. The minimum number is three. The minimum number of non-speaking soldiers is two. Some parts may be doubled: Beatrice Kastoria can be played by a valley woman, as can the Brother, since he isn't seen. One actor can play The Doctor, Father Gabriel, Philip Kastoria and Alonso. One actor can play the Narrator and the Lieutenant. Or perhaps the Lieutenant can be played by the same actor who plays Alonso.

ACT ONE

Scene 1

The women by the river, washing clothes.

TERESA. The baby won't speak?

YANINA. Not a word.

TERESA. He's how old?

YANINA. Old enough to talk.

KATHERINA. Good that he's quiet, he'll stay out of trouble.

TERESA. He has to talk sometime . . .

KATHERINA. Not if he knows what's good for him.

ROSA. There's something wrong with the water today.

ALEXANDRA. You say that every day.

ROSA. Nothing's coming clean.

MARILUZ. Whisper to him.

ALEXANDRA (*to* ROSA). You just don't scrub hard enough.

MARILUZ. Whisper. Right in his ear.

KATHERINA. That baby misses his papa.

YANINA. He never saw his papa.

Little pause.

FIDELIA. I'll whisper to him.

TERESA. Work his tongue with your fingers, a little each day.

YANINA. Fidelia tells him stories.

ALEXANDRA. Instead of doing her chores.

FIDELIA. Mama . . .

ROSA. There is. There's something strange about the water today.

YANINA. He's a sad baby.

KATHERINA. You think he knows that his papa is . . .

TERESA. Ssshhhh . . .

YANINA. He knows what I know.

A little pause, then FATHER GABRIEL *enters, breathlessly.*

FATHER GABRIEL. Everyone come, it's time, it's time!

He exits.

CECILIA (*entering*). The jeep just pulled up. The new captain's here . . .

The WOMEN *stare at* CECILIA. *An icy silence.*

CECILIA. It's a big jeep.

She exits.

The WOMEN *put down their washing, wring dry wet things, load everything into baskets and, whispering to each other, exit.* SOFIA *is left alone, sitting by the river.* FIDELIA *re-enters.*

FIDELIA. Grandma, don't you want to see . . . ?

ALEXANDRA *re-enters dragging* ALEXIS.

ALEXANDRA (*to* ALEXIS). Stay with your Grandma.

ALEXIS. I want to see the new Captain. I want to see what he looks like.

ALEXANDRA. I don't want him to see what you look like. I'm a smart woman. Why did I have such stupid children? Fidelia . . .

FIDELIA. Grandma, they said this Captain – he's bringing news. Don't you . . .

ALEXANDRA. Fidelia, come. (*To* SOFIA.) You've turned everything upside down. The others think you've gone crazy and my children don't listen to me now.

ALEXANDRA *and* FIDELIA *exit. A little pause.* ALEXIS *looks at the silent old woman, who watches the river expectantly.*

ALEXIS. Grandma . . . ?

Are you crazy?

SOFIA. Yes.

ALEXIS. When did you go crazy?

SOFIA. Do I scare you?

ALEXIS. No.

SOFIA. Little rabbit.

ALEXIS. I'm not. I'm a man.

SOFIA. Not yet. Lucky.

The CAPTAIN *enters, on foot, following a surveyor's map; under his arm, plans and designs in plastic tubes.*

CAPTAIN (*to* ALEXIS). You, boy, can you tell me if . . .

ALEXIS *runs away.*

CAPTAIN. Come back here, I . . . damn. (*To* SOFIA.) Excuse me, Mrs . . . uh . . . I'm trying to . . .

SOFIA *shows no sign of being aware of his presence.*

CAPTAIN. Is this the bend where the women do their washing? (*Picks up a piece of clothing.*) Must be.

I thought it would be greener.

We're going to build here. Big plant. For fertilizer manufacturing.

The OLD WOMAN *mutters, shifts her skirts.*

CAPTAIN. What? Did you . . . Are you from around here, your husband, does he ever talk about fertilizer? Well, I think you just have to look at how arid it all is, to see . . . it's poor soil nutrients, that's why . . . Does your husband ever express the need for modern fertilizers for his land?

SOFIA. No.

CAPTAIN. Oh.

Well I think fertilizer would. . . help. The army's going to build a plant here, then he'll see what he's missing. Your husband. Bigger crops. Exports. Are you . . . What are you doing here? Are you waiting for someone?

SOFIA. Yes.

CAPTAIN (*introducing himself*). I'm . . .

SOFIA. I'm waiting for my father.

CAPTAIN. Your father.

SOFIA. And my husband.

CAPTAIN. How old is your father?

SOFIA. And my sons.

CAPTAIN. Your father must be at least . . .

SOFIA. Old.

CAPTAIN. Been waiting long?

Little pause. She looks at him.

SOFIA. The others. They all ran off to the village. To have a look at you.

She laughs, a small, dry, sly laugh. It makes him uncomfortable at first, then he gets it, and he laughs too. Then she stops laughing.

SOFIA. All of us. We have all been waiting a long time.

Scene 2

A light comes up on an empty chair on the other side of the stage. After a few seconds, the NARRATOR *steps into the spotlight. He talks directly to the audience.*

NARRATOR. It was when I was in exile. That's when. I couldn't get to sleep at night. I would wait for silence, for all the foreign noises of the foreign country I was living in to die down. I would wait for the children in the apartment next door to go to bed so their voices wouldn't remind me that they were not my children, that my children were far away. I would wait for their parents and every other mother and father in the neighbourhood to stop arguing to the death in that language I still could not understand but which everybody for miles and miles around me spoke. I would wait for the stars to darken so I wouldn't have to see them, be reminded of how different the stars were back home. Even the bitching constellations were my enemies. That's when. When even the dogs had stopped barking in the way that dogs bark when you are far from your country and you cannot sleep. My country? Does it matter? Do I really have to name that country? Among all the countries – the ones you see on television and the many you don't – where a few men decide the life and the death of the rest of the people, a few men decide that one man shall disappear, that another man shall go into exile and never see his children again. Do I really have to name it? Just like the country where a river flows and an old woman waits – do you really need me to name that country?

Scene 3

The CAPTAIN *and* EMMANUEL.

EMMANUEL. Did you find the bend in the river, sir?

CAPTAIN. Of course I did. I can read a map. And the river's not exactly a mystery to follow.

EMMANUEL. I'm supposed to drive you, sir, that's my job.

CAPTAIN. I'll let you know what your job is, Orderly.

EMMANUEL. Yes sir.

CAPTAIN. When I want to walk, I'll walk. Understood?

EMMANUEL. As you say, sir.

CAPTAIN. Good.

You're from around here, aren't you?

EMMANUEL. On the other side of the hill, Captain. Forty miles from here.

CAPTAIN. So you understand these people?

EMMANUEL. Sort of, Captain.

CAPTAIN. Sort of. Captain Urqueta said you knew your way around.

EMMANUEL. I'm different from them, Captain. I was employed by Mr. Kastoria, I know better. With your permission, sir, I don't think I'll stay here my whole life. I'd like to . . .

CAPTAIN. I met an old woman. Tough old bitch. By the river. I got the impression she was expecting someone on a . . . raft, or something . . .

EMMANUEL. Old Sofia. The Fuentes woman.

CAPTAIN. You know her?

EMMANUEL. She sits by the river all day, sir. Has for months. Probably a little . . . (*Indicates 'crazy'.*)

She told you she was waiting for her men?

CAPTAIN. I could barely get a word out of her.

Her father and her husband and . . .

EMMANUEL. Her sons. A lot of the men in the valley are . . . they're gone, sir.

CAPTAIN. Gone.

EMMANUEL. Disappeared, they . . .

CAPTAIN. Arrested?

How many men in all are missing?

EMMANUEL. All, sir.

CAPTAIN. All? *All* the men?

EMMANUEL. I . . . think you should speak to the Lieutenant, sir.

CAPTAIN. *All* the men? That wasn't mentioned in the briefing.

Pause.

In my other jurisdictions I kept a lid on that – making men vanish like that – it's no good. It drives the women out of their minds. Even if you give them a finger to bury, but when there's just nothing . . . They go crazy. And then the world does.

Hard times.

EMMANUEL. Yes sir.

CAPTAIN. She has a little moustache.

EMMANUEL. Sir?

CAPTAIN. I hate women with moustaches.

Looking out the window.

Her whole family?

EMMANUEL. All the men.

CAPTAIN. I suppose then we'll have to forgive her . . . her moustache. Won't we?

FATHER GABRIEL (*entering*) We're glad you finally made it, Captain. We'd heard you were lost.

CAPTAIN. Who told you that, Father?

FATHER GABRIEL. Oh, in Camacho we end up knowing everything, Captain. But the women are waiting.

CAPTAIN. Women waiting. We don't want that.

Scene 4

The CAPTAIN *is addressing the women. He is alone on stage and talks to the audience.*

CAPTAIN. The war is over: in the cities, in the mountains, in this valley. What remains is the national task of building a deep and true peace, the peace that brings prosperity. But in the memories of some, the war goes on.

Terrible, strict measures have been necessary; we have all suffered great loss, the people and its army.

Those of us with determination and courage for the future are ready to let go. We are ready to forgive your disobedience if you are willing to forget our stern response to it, if you learn to behave.

If you join us, if you are prepared to forget the past, the wounds may finally begin to heal. Democracy and technology will be brought to bear on your backwardness, fertilizer plants and animal husbandry, pesticides and . . . and libraries; a new land for a new people. And if you let us, we will bring your sorrow and great loneliness to an end.

Scene 5

SOFIA *at the river, alone.*

SOFIA (*to the river*). What are you bringing me? I'm an old woman. I can't be expected to wait much longer.

FIDELIA *enters running.*

FIDELIA. They're coming home, they're coming home!

ALEXANDRA (*entering*). Sofia, where's Alexis?

Little pause.

Sofia? Where's . . .

SOFIA (*dazed, looking about*). I don't know, he was here, he must have gone home.

ALEXANDRA. Oh Sofia, you were supposed to watch him.

FIDELIA. I thought he was supposed to watch her.

ALEXANDRA. Quiet. ALEXIS!

She exits, calling his name.

ALEXIS!

FIDELIA. Papa's coming back, grandma, everyone's excited, they . . .

TERESA *appears, shucking corn. She's there but not there.*

TERESA. Fidelia, don't tell lies.

FIDELIA stops, looks at her, then:

FIDELIA. I'm not lying, the new captain, he said the men are coming . . .

TERESA. He said maybe. If we behave . . .

KATHERINA (*appearing, mending clothes*). If we behave.

YANINA *enters.*

FIDELIA. But we behave already, all we do is behave, we . . .

TERESA. Sofia doesn't.

KATHERINA. Sitting by the river all day . . .

TERESA. She doesn't behave.

YANINA. Take the baby, my arms are tired.

YANINA *gives the baby to* FIDELIA.

ALEXANDRA (*calling off*). ALEXIS!

YANINA. You should have come, Sofia, the new captain met with us, he spoke to us, he said . . .

TERESA. Forget the past.

KATHERINA. Bury the past.

ROSA (*appearing, stirring a pot*). Let go the dead.

TERESA. He didn't say that.

KATHERINA. He never mentioned the dead.

YANINA. He promised us, Sofia, if we co-operate, he said . . . maybe we can't trust him, if you'd been there, you could tell us, if you'd seen him . . .

SOFIA. I saw him.

ROSA. Listen to her, she lies worse than her granddaughter.

SOFIA. Mind your business . . .

ROSA. It is my business, he said behave.

SOFIA. He said fertilizer plant. I know what he said.

YANINA. But you were here the whole time. How, how did you . . . ?

SOFIA. Go home, Yanina, it's almost dusk, put the nets on the baskets or the grasshoppers will crawl out of the ground and eat the grain.

YANINA. I did that already.

FIDELIA. I helped her, grandma, we . . .

SOFIA. You probably did it wrong. You put the nets on all anyhow and the grasshoppers slip through.

KATHERINA. Full of advice, criticizing everyone, but she hasn't worked in a month. Give yourself some advice, Sofia, act your age . . .

TERESA. Sitting there . . .

ROSA. Like a river rock . . .

KATHERINA. Stubborn, bitter, a tombstone . . .

ROSA. Reproachful . . .

TERESA. As if to say that we've forgotten the . . .

ROSA (*crossing herself*). Sssshhh.

TERESA. That's why you can't brood. You'll lose your mind, you'll turn to stone.

ALEXANDRA (*still off*). ALEXIS!

ROSA. When they took the land away from us, and we had to watch the fences go up again, and . . . and smile. You whispered to me, like a promise, Sofia, life goes on, like the earth, no matter what. Now get up.

SOFIA. I can't. I'm carrying the weight of my four men. I have a father. Husband. Two sons. Where? Each one is heavy. Each time I think of him, is he hungry, does he need water, is he cold, he gets heavier. I am a stone. Where are they? Where are my men? I remember the missing so sharply I've forgotten everything else, how to bake or plant or walk or even stand. I can't move. I'm waiting here because . . .

ALEXANDRA *enters, dragging* ALEXIS.

FIDELIA. Grandma? Because . . . ?

SOFIA. I'm waiting. Because I can't bear waiting anymore.

ALEXANDRA. I'm tired of this. We're going home.

FIDELIA. Grandma.

ALEXANDRA. Leave her. On the ground there like an animal.

(*To* SOFIA.) They're watching and you know it. You call attention to yourself. To all of us.

ALEXANDRA *begins to exit with* FIDELIA. ALEXIS *tries to stay behind to talk with* SOFIA.

ALEXIS (*to* SOFIA). I had to run, mama told me not to let . . .

ALEXANDRA *pulls* ALEXIS, *they leave with* YANINA *and* FIDELIA. SOFIA *sits alone. All the women disappear except* TERESA.

SOFIA. Don't you feel something . . .

TERESA. Feel what?

SOFIA. Something is coming.

TERESA. No.

SOFIA. Something is.

Little pause.

TERESA. When my husband comes back, he'd better find me tending the fields and feeding the children and selling the crops at market. I wait too, but not like this, Sofia, not like this.

She exits.

SOFIA (*puts her hand in the river*). Something is. It's almost here.

Scene 6

CECILIA *and* EMMANUEL *by the river; he's trying to make love to her.*

CECILIA. Not here.

EMMANUEL. I love this place. Green.

CECILIA. I hate green.

EMMANUEL. Even before I knew you, this place reminded me of you. I knew someday I'd be here with you.

CECILIA. I used to come here with . . . (*She stops.*)

EMMANUEL. Say who.

CECILIA. Let's go.

EMMANUEL. Theo. (*Calling, teasing her.*) Hey, Theo!

CECILIA. Stop it.

He's coming back. Everybody says . . .

EMMANUEL. Stupid bitches.

CECILIA. The captain told them. I heard him.

EMMANUEL. He never said . . .

CECILIA. All the women, they're getting their beds ready . . .

EMMANUEL. Then there are going to be a lot of disappointed women in cold beds around here – except for one little sweet woman I know. She's luckier . . .

He gropes her, she pulls away.

CECILIA. Those witches. They hate me because we're in love. They'll tell Theo.

EMMANUEL. You're protected.

Grabbing his uniform.

You know what this is?

Grabbing his pistol.

You know what this is?

What's he got? Your husband? Even if he did come back he won't but say he did? See those trees?

CECILIA. Yes.

EMMANUEL. I love those trees. Try to touch the fruit on those trees someone you don't even see will shoot your hand off. Green Kastoria land. Protected.

When I was a kid I'd come here, I'd walk six hours, I watched for birds.

CECILIA. Did you climb over and steal the fruit?

EMMANUEL. Not me. I watched for the birds, if they tried to land in the fruit trees, I threw pebbles at them and scared them off. I knew even then I was supposed to protect his property – that that was what I was born for. Mr. Kastoria didn't know I was alive and if I'd climbed over the fence they'd've shot me but I was proud to be protecting what was his.

My father used to beat me. He knew where I'd been and when I got back he beat the shit out of me.

CECILIA. Poor baby.

EMMANUEL. Do you know what a war is?

CECILIA. I know what a war is. Yes.

EMMANUEL. You take sides and if you lose, you're fucked.

'They stole the land from our people.' That's what he said when he beat me with the belt, 'they drove us into the mountains,' he said and he'd belt me, 'now we have to come and pick their fruit,' and he would . . . He was right to beat me. My father knew I was his enemy.

One day I just didn't come back. Mr. Kastoria rode out of the gate on a big white horse and asked me if I wanted to work for him. Know what he said?

CECILIA. No.

EMMANUEL. He said, 'You've got to shoot the birds that eat the fruit. That way they won't come back.' And he handed me a gun.

My father must have waited for me all day, with his strap in his hand, watching the horizon. I never went home again.

The CAPTAIN *and the* LIEUTENANT *standing atop a hill nearby.*

LIEUTENANT. You know what I love about this country, Captain? Its quality of timelessness. One man is born a peasant, over there, in the dust, and his son will be and his son will be, and if you allow it there's a deep satisfaction, a calm, that comes from that. And on this side, the green fertile side, the transfer of property through the generations. My father and his father and his father . . . The Fourteen Families: For four hundred years we have cultivated a loving relationship to the land, gentle and subtle, making it produce for all. There is a deep, an inevitable structure in the world, a Holy Structure, if you will. So it is also inevitable that the people of the dust will always covet the green; if they get ideas, feel encouraged to lay hold of the green, everything, everything decent and beautiful and civilized, gets covered in dust. As we have seen in the last eight years.

CAPTAIN. And you are telling me this. . . ?

LIEUTENANT. Back in town with the women yesterday, I don't mean any disrespect, Captain, but that was a very nice speech you made. Democracy. Fertilizers.

CAPTAIN. I'm getting into the habit of making speeches. I'm good at it.

LIEUTENANT. It was a very nice speech. Of course not the speech I'd've made.

If I was Captain. But I'm not.

CAPTAIN. But if you were . . . you'd have spoken of. . . dust?

LIEUTENANT. In a way. I'd've said: 'Congratulations. You're alive. Want to stay that way?' Captain. We can't give the impression we're weak.

Pause.

CAPTAIN. Lieutenant, back in Chipote, a few years ago, I ordered my battalion to fire on a crowd in the village square. I stood and watched that. When it was dark I took my flashlight and

I searched among the bodies in the square. There was so much blood it seeped into my boots. There was a nine-year-old kid. So young. His arm was . . . You know. I stood there and watched him die. It took an hour. The boots dried while I watched. And then the flashlight burnt out.

Weak men die from nights like that. I'm not a weak man. But . . . I am tired. The war is over.

LIEUTENANT. Over.

You see down there by that bend in the river. Looks like a flyspeck, but it's an old woman.

CAPTAIN. Old Mrs. Fuentes.

LIEUTENANT. You think . . . it's over for her? Go on, tell her that. Just be sure you're carrying a gun.

It's taken us eight years to restore order. And it's our duty to ensure that we never have to restore order again. So you never have to watch a little boy die like that ever again. So I never have to watch what I have watched.

CAPTAIN. No order without progress.

If you want to keep order you have to pull them out of their poverty, their dust. We have to move forward.

LIEUTENANT. And you will wind up right back here again. Looking at the green, at the dust, at that old woman. Timelessness. The past awaits you, Captain.

CECILIA. Times are changing, Emmanuel. Maybe we could go see your family. Make it up with your father.

EMMANUEL. He . . . He's a loser.

Doesn't matter.

CECILIA. Why not? It matters to me.

EMMANUEL. They took him. Disappeared. Like Theo. And he's never coming back.

Scene 7

Late at night at the riverbend. SOFIA, FIDELIA *and* ALEXIS.

SOFIA. Here, where the river thinks of going one way and then goes another – this is where they died.

ALEXIS. Who killed them?

SOFIA. You know this story.

FIDELIA *and* ALEXIS. Tell us again, Grandma.

SOFIA. The Spanish. My great-great-great grandfather and his
wife. She was fierce. The Spanish believed she ate the eyeballs
of her enemies . . .

FIDELIA. Did she?

SOFIA. I hope so.

I light these candles for their little souls. This water saw them
die. The water watches everything, it flows everywhere, and
when I am lost, or when I've lost something, I know the water
will help me find it.

You have to know how to ask it.

She strikes a match, lights first one candle, then another.

Now these little souls will watch over me, and you go home to
bed. Go my babies, if your mother wakes up and finds you
missing . . .

*In the surrounding darkness, a lit candle is seen – it appears to
float . . .*

ALEXIS. Grandma, is that . . .

SOFIA. Sssshhh. Who is that? Who's there?

The river grows more audible.

TERESA (*entering*). I can't sleep at nights with you here, all I do
is watch you . . .

SOFIA. You live miles from here . . .

TERESA. From the window, by my door . . . I heard the floor-
boards creak and it was Antonio, I thought it was Antonio, it's
the same dream, every night since you started sitting here, it's
my husband, but he won't talk to me, and it's you, Sofia, you're
disturbing him, wherever they've got him, go home, let me rest.

KATHERINA (*entering*). I heard Roberto calling out to me and I
ran out the door to greet him and the yard was empty and I saw
these candles. I want to sleep, Sofia, without dreaming. Leave
the night alone.

SOFIA. I have dreams too.

I can see my hand, and in my hand there's a needle and a
thread, and I'm sewing something, I look down to see, and it's
a mouth I'm sewing, I'm sewing it shut, and it's eyelids I'm

sewing, and human ears, all familiar somehow, and there's no blood on the needle and no blood on the thread and on my fingers it's . . . and I've sewed him into a bundle, a tight white bundle, he's calling to me, I hear him, I fear he may be dead but oh God let him be alive.

The sound of the river grows terribly loud. ROSA *enters.*

ROSA. What's wrong with the water, what's wrong with the river, why is it making such a terrible noise, what have you done, Sofia, what are you doing to the water in the river? You're clouding the river, the clothes won't come clean, leave the river alone . . .

FIDELIA. Grandma, what is it, what's the matter with the river?

TERESA. There's something in the water, there's something in the water, get a line, get a hook . . .

ROSA. The children, get the children away from the . . .

SOFIA. Alexis, Fidelia, get away from the river . . .

The WOMEN *begin to wade into the river; the sound of the current grows louder still. The* WOMEN *whisper the following, or maybe we hear it whispered urgently on tape:*

TERESA. Careful careful, don't slip, he . . .

ROSA. Grab the sleeve, grab the . . .

SOFIA. On the rocks, he's caught on the rocks, pull, pull . . .

TERESA. Pull, pull . . .

SOFIA. Now lift. Gently.

The WOMEN, *soaking wet, pull the body from the river. Immediately the sound of the current softens, grows calm.*

SOFIA. Ooohhhh. I knew it.

Silence. MARILUZ *enters. Behind her, the other women.*

MARILUZ. Oh God. Oh God it's not . . .

TERESA. It doesn't look like anyone.

SOFIA. I knew, I knew . . .

ROSA. Children don't look. Sofia, it's not . . . It hasn't got a face.

Pause.

SOFIA. Fidelia, go get the priest. And bring a shovel.

ALEXIS. Who is it, Grandma?

SOFIA. It's my father.

TERESA. It's not your . . . It isn't, Sofia.

SOFIA. It is.

TERESA. You can't bury that.

SOFIA. Not here. He has a place, by my mother. In the cemetery on the hill.

ROSA. You need permission.

SOFIA. Not for this.

TERESA. The captain said behave.

AMANDA. For God's sake, Sofia, you know you need permission.

LUCIA. We can't make trouble now.

ROSA. They have our men.

FIDELIA. Grandma, if Papa were. . . if my Papa. . .

Pause.

SOFIA. No trouble. Yes. Permission.

It is my father.

She starts to leave.

ALEXIS. Wait. I'll go with you.

Pause.

SOFIA. Aren't you afraid?

ALEXIS. No.

SOFIA. You should be.

Come.

ROSA. You can't take the boy, are you out of your . . .

FIDELIA. Grandma, mama will be angry if . . .

SOFIA. This is how it should be. His father would accompany me. Emiliano. If he was here. This is how the Fuentes bury their dead.

KATHERINA. The Fuentes should protect their children.

SOFIA. No one can protect him anymore. No one touches this body. You understand?

FIDELIA. Yes, grandma.

SOFIA. Alexis, come.

Nothing to fear. This Captain is different. Right?

TERESA. You'd better hope so.

SOFIA. *You* hope. I'm going to bury my father.

They exit. The remaining WOMEN *watch the body.* YANINA *enters.*

YANINA. I woke up, I couldn't sleep, I . . .

She sees the body.

Oh. Oh. Oh God.

Little pause.

Who?

Scene 8

The light on the NARRATOR *and the empty chair comes on.*

NARRATOR. Exile is like death. Among the Guarani Indians of Paraguay, when someone is banished from the community, they say he has died. And when he returns, if he returns that is, they say he has come back from the dead. They celebrate the return of the exile as if he had been resurrected.

If he is resurrected.

If he hasn't faded from people's lives, from the eyes of his son, from the lips of his daughter.

People speak of him in hushed voices, in the past tense. If they speak of him at all.

But that's not what I wanted to tell you.

I wanted to tell you that today I met a woman publisher from my country. She was passing through this foreign city where I now live, passing on her way back from a Book Fair or something. We had been lovers – maybe that had been ten years ago – and she was as ravishing as ever.

Over lunch, she asked me what I was doing. I told her I was thinking about a story. I didn't tell her I was haunted by it, that I couldn't get it out of my head, that it was like a mother rescuing me from madness. I just told her what it was about. And added, about when dessert was served, that maybe she could help me get the story to our country, publish it under a pseudonym, I said to her.

I could tell she thought I was crazy. I could see it in her eyes. I saw what she saw: her books burnt, the soldiers breaking down the door, her interrogation. I saw it deep inside her. The fear for her own children.

But what if I made things easy for you. What if I disguised this story, set it in Greece, say, under the Nazi occupation, or in Nigeria or Guatemala or Iraq, you pick the country I said to her – we'll set it there, and then we'll make up a foreign author, we'll attribute the story to him, to her, nobody will know that this was thought up by somebody like me, nobody will know that it refers to our country.

If she hadn't said yes immediately, that she would do it, I might have some hope now. But I know when a woman is lying. She said yes too quickly. A way of getting rid of me.

Oh, I'll send it to her when it's done, when I've figured out how all this ends, I'll write it under a false name, I'll set it in East Timor or South Africa or Roumania or anywhere else that she wants, but it won't be any use.

The bitch didn't even invite me back to her hotel room.

For her, it's as if I had already died.

Scene 9

Very early dawn. The doctor stands near the river, smoking. The women in a group, near the body. The LIEUTENANT *enters with soldiers.*

LIEUTENANT. Full of surprises, this river. I don't suppose anyone's moved the body, right?

Pause.

Yes or no?

The women shake their heads no.

And which one of you found it?

The women make an inclusive gesture; they all found it.

DOCTOR. He's dead, no doubt about it.

LIEUTENANT. I was hoping you could provide us with more specific information, Doctor.

The DOCTOR *gestures to a* SOLDIER, *indicates how he wants the body turned. The* SOLDIER *turns the corpse over.*

LIEUTENANT (*to* TERESA). You found the body?

Pause.

Answer. Did you find it?

TERESA. Yes sir. Along with the others, sir.

LIEUTENANT. Recognize it?

TERESA *doesn't answer. She looks at the body. The* LIEUTENANT *turns to* AMANDA.

LIEUTENANT. Did you look at his face?

AMANDA *shakes her head, backs away.*

LIEUTENANT. I asked you a question. Jesus Christ, were you people born deaf?

(*To the* DOCTOR.) Take the pants off.

DOCTOR. This is only a preliminary . . .

LIEUTENANT. It'll help to identify him.

RAMONA. We didn't want to.

LIEUTENANT. You didn't want to see his face?

RAMONA. No sir.

LIEUTENANT (*to the doctor*). Take off the goddamn pants.

Pause. The SOLDIERS *take off the corpse's pants.*

LIEUTENANT. So?

DOCTOR. Burns, contusions, broken bones – a disaster. It looks to me like he was given a good beating before they dumped him in. He was hungry too. Look at these ribs.

LIEUTENANT. I think the river is responsible.

DOCTOR. For the burns?

LIEUTENANT. I don't see burns. Look closer.

DOCTOR. I already told you what I think. But if you think differently . . .

LIEUTENANT. Any clues about the subject's identity? Age?

DOCTOR. I can't tell the age. He seems to have been away from the sun months, years perhaps. A peasant. Look at those hands – of course they're broken now, the . . . river, I suppose.

LIEUTENANT. And in the pockets?

DOCTOR. Nothing.

LIEUTENANT (*to the* WOMEN). You women. I want you to pass by this body, one by one, and take a good look at the face. A formal identification process.

Everything nice and proper for the new citizens of the new land.

The WOMEN *do this, except* FIDELIA.

KATHERINA. It could be my brother, sir. They took him away four years ago.

LIEUTENANT. Your brother? Are you sure? (*Pause.*)

KATHERINA. How could I be sure? How could I want this to be my brother?

LIEUTENANT. I wouldn't want it to be mine.

Good. The people have spoken, or rather not spoken.

He gestures to SOLDIERS *to cart the body away. When they move towards it* FIDELIA *goes right to the body.*

LIEUTENANT. Well well. Re-enforcements . . .

FIDELIA. It's my great-grandfather.

The LIEUTENANT *looks at her in a frankly sexual way for a long time.*

TERESA. Ignore her, sir, she's a little strange.

LIEUTENANT. Your great-grandfather. Oh my. And what's your pretty name?

FIDELIA. Fidelia Fuentes.

LIEUTENANT. Emiliano's daughter?

FIDELIA. Yes. This is my great-grandfather. Carlos Mendez.

LIEUTENANT. And you identified him just like that, girl, from a distance?

FIDELIA. My grandma Sofia identified him, sir.

LIEUTENANT. Strange she's not here. We didn't think grandma could move. We thought she was screwed to the spot.

And where might she be now? Would you happen to know that?

Before answering FIDELIA *moves hesitantly to the corpse, sits beside it, and takes one of its hands in hers.*

FIDELIA. She went to the captain, sir. To ask permission to bury her father.

LIEUTENANT. She's wasting her time.

Pause.

Now get away from that body.

Pause. FIDELIA *doesn't move.*

LIEUTENANT. Don't fuck with me, girl.

Pause. The LIEUTENANT *and the* SOLDIERS *watch* FIDELIA, *who doesn't respond, doesn't move. The* WOMEN *stand at a distance, but not too far.*

TERESA. Leave her be, sir. I told you she's strange.

YANINA. Fidelia, come.

LIEUTENANT. You're the wife of . . . Alonso, right? I'm good at remembering names.

YANINA. Fidelia!

FIDELIA. My grandma never wastes time, sir. She doesn't believe in that.

The LIEUTENANT *goes to* FIDELIA, *grabs her by the shoulders, picks her up with great strength but complete control, and moves her away from the body. He kisses her violently, lets her go. Then he motions to the soldiers. They pick up the body, carry it out.*

DOCTOR. I need a drink.

LIEUTENANT. There's the river. Don't fall in.

He exits. The WOMEN *remain, immobile.*

Scene 10

The CAPTAIN's *office, the* CAPTAIN, EMMANUEL, SOFIA *and* ALEXIS.

CAPTAIN. You're sure about this.

SOFIA. Yes.

CAPTAIN. This drowned man is your father. You're sure?

SOFIA. Yes.

CAPTAIN. Why would an old man like that have gotten mixed up with politics?

SOFIA. He didn't.

CAPTAIN. Well, you said he was arrested. For what?

SOFIA. For nothing.

CAPTAIN. Mrs. Fuentes, people don't get arrested for nothing, they . . .

To EMMANUEL:

Emmanuel, did you know this man? Mendez.

EMMANUEL. Yes sir.

CAPTAIN. Well . . . ?

Little pause. EMMANUEL *very uncomfortable under* SOFIA's *stare.*

CAPTAIN (*slightly impatient*). Orderly?

EMMANUEL. Mendez, her father, went around to houses and churches and places where the men would drink and . . . talked about land. Mr. Kastoria's land. He was angry when we . . . moved them off the land. Fuentes her husband also. First and mostly her father. The files say he is no longer in custody.

CAPTAIN (*to* SOFIA). Perhaps you're confused.

SOFIA. No.

CAPTAIN. Perhaps your father ran way, or . . .

SOFIA. No.

CAPTAIN. He might have had an accident, or . . . well, sometimes men run away for . . .

SOFIA. He could barely walk.

CAPTAIN. Women make men do strange things.

SOFIA. He was eighty years old.

CAPTAIN. Or sometimes terrorists have business to settle amongst themselves . . .

SOFIA. No, he wasn't a violent man. He wasn't a . . .

CAPTAIN. Well he must have been doing something. Stop interrupting me.

He reaches in his desk, takes out a sheet of paper.

This is the new amnesty decree. Do you know what amnesty is? Am-nes-ty. If your father or your husband . . .

SOFIA. Or my sons.

CAPTAIN. Or whoever. Has been in trouble with the government, now they can surrender. Without inconvenience. So maybe they'll come back to you from wherever they're hiding. What would your father think if he came back and found you burying him? Hmm?

She picks up the paper, examines it like a strange object, turning it over and over, and then putting it back carefully on his desk.

SOFIA. I've come for permission to bury my father.

CAPTAIN. Yes, yes we established that, we know that, you said that already, now have you heard a single word I . . .

SOFIA. He came to me . . . from the land of the dead. His body. Because he wanted me to bury him. Where all the dead of our family are buried. In the cemetery on the hill. He came back to his daughter for that. Give me permission.

There is a knock on the door. The LIEUTENANT enters.

LIEUTENANT. I'd like to speak with you for a moment, sir, if . . .

CAPTAIN. Of course, I . . . Lieutenant, you know Mrs. Fuentes? And this is her grandson . . . mmmm . . .

LIEUTENANT. Alexis.

CAPTAIN. Alexis. Right.

Mrs. Fuentes, I'm a reasonable man. Pending the results of the official inquest, this body, if it can be established that it really is your father . . .

SOFIA. Carlos Mendez.

CAPTAIN. If it is . . . Carlos Mendez, then you will naturally be allowed to bury him. The army is the servant of the people.

SOFIA. I'll wait.

CAPTAIN. It may take . . .

SOFIA. I'll wait.

SOFIA takes ALEXIS by the hand and exits. The CAPTAIN snaps his fingers at EMMANUEL, who follows them out.

CAPTAIN. She never blinks.

Crazy old bitch. Makes me nervous. After the inquest . . .

LIEUTENANT. Inquest.

CAPTAIN. Give her the body. Quickest way to get rid of her.

LIEUTENANT. You're joking.

Inquest? Give her the . . . You're joking.

CAPTAIN. I don't think I am.

LIEUTENANT. And what do we do after the funeral?

CAPTAIN. After the . . . ?

LIEUTENANT. When she wants to know: who killed him.

Little pause.

No evidence.

CAPTAIN. What do you mean, no . . .

LIEUTENANT. No evidence.

CAPTAIN. Where's the body, Lieutenant?

The LIEUTENANT *picks up a pinch of ash from the ashtray, blows it into the air.*

LIEUTENANT. Gone.

CAPTAIN. You . . .

LIEUTENANT. Burned it.

Sorry.

CAPTAIN. You . . . You *burned* the . . . How dare you, how fucking *dare* you, I gave you orders to bring that corpse back to . . . You BURNED it? That is a flagrant violation of my orders, of proper military procedure, you . . .

LIEUTENANT. What are you talking about? Excuse me, sir, but what are you . . . Proper military . . .

Listen to yourself. Somewhere right now somewhere else in this country, maybe your last command, someone is losing a piece of paper, erasing a signature, burning a body to cover your ass. And you . . . cover mine. That's how the army's going to survive in your new democratic paradise. I cover you, you cover me.

CAPTAIN. You killed him? Her father? You . . .

LIEUTENANT. I arrested him.

CAPTAIN. And you . . .

LIEUTENANT. Let him go the next day. What happened after that . . . is not for us to say.

CAPTAIN. Mother of God. You burned the . . .

What do I tell her? That old bitch out there with that stupid kid, for Christ sake, what do I say to her?

LIEUTENANT. Say there's no body. Say there never was a body. Say 'Fuck off you old bitch'.

The CAPTAIN *goes to the office door, opens it, sees the* OLD WOMAN *sitting outside, and closes the door.*

CAPTAIN. She's waiting out there.

LIEUTENANT. Don't tell her anything.

CAPTAIN. Well I can't just . . . let her wait. She'll wait forever.

LIEUTENANT. Not forever. She's an old woman. You'll probably outlive her.

End of Act One.

ACT TWO

Scene 11

ALEXANDRA *and* YANINA *are pounding grain,* FIDELIA *pouring it into sacks.*

ALEXANDRA. Pour it slower, you spill half on the ground.

FIDELIA. I'm not spilling anything.

ALEXANDRA. Don't talk back to me.

YANINA. You're spilling, Alexandra, you're pounding too hard, half of it's coming over the sides . . .

ALEXANDRA. I can't believe she took Alexis.

(*To* FIDELIA.) I can't believe she left you to guard that thing. I can't believe you touched it, you're so dumb, it's unclean. Did you wash your hands? Did you wash your mouth?

FIDELIA. You asked me already, I said I did, stop yelling at me, I . . .

ALEXANDRA (*overlapping with above*). I can still smell it, I don't think you washed enough, you'll get that death in the grain, I . . .

YANINA (*overlapping with above*). You'll wake the baby, please stop . . .

SOFIA *and* ALEXIS *enter.* ALEXANDRA *immediately stops talking and begins pounding even harder.* ALEXIS *heads for the house.*

ALEXANDRA (*to* ALEXIS). You. Stay.

Little pause. Pounding.

SOFIA (*to* ALEXANDRA, *very tightly controlled rage*). You're pounding too hard.

ALEXANDRA *pounds even harder.*

You'll crack the bowl, stop pounding so . . .

ALEXANDRA. Don't. Talk. To. Me.

SOFIA. That bowl you are breaking is my bowl and I won't let you . . .

ALEXANDRA. Nothing here is yours, it's yours if you work it and you, you haven't done any work in a month, and now it isn't yours any more, it's mine, my bowl, my house, my goat and chickens and grain and . . . and MY children and you . . . just go back to the river and leave me and what's mine, all the things you don't care for anymore!

SOFIA (*very quiet*). There were four goats when I left a month ago and now there are only three. How much did you get for Cholito?

ALEXANDRA. You know what I can't forgive? It's not disgracing your father's name by giving it to a rotting corpse, it's not being a crazy old woman who can't help herself because crazy old women can't help the way they are, what I cannot forgive, ever, is that you . . .

SOFIA. I asked you a question.

ALEXANDRA (*barely controlling herself*). What.

SOFIA. How much money did you get for the goat?

ALEXANDRA (*quietly*). You put my daughter and my son in danger.

I thought . . . the one thing I could depend on was that you cared about my children. Your grandchildren. That you would protect them. You care about nothing but death.

FIDELIA. No, mama, that's not true, she . . .

SOFIA. Fidelia. What did I tell you when I left you at the river?

FIDELIA. Grandma, I . . .

SOFIA. I entrusted you with the body of my father. And you let those godless men take my father's body and they burned it, like trash, and you let them do that.

ALEXANDRA. Don't talk to my daughter like . . .

SOFIA. She should have died before she let them take his body away! Forgive! I don't forgive any of you for that! (*To* ALEXANDRA.) You have no Mendez blood in your veins, no Fuentes blood, you don't understand, but you, (*To* FIDELIA.) I thought you were Emiliano's daughter, but you understand nothing, none of you, I come back and you're going to market, my father's body, he built this house, black smoke and ash and you're going to market, you'll sell the living, you'll sell the dead, nothing's horrible enough to stop your selling, and your pounding, any of you, any of you in this whole valley, you bitches, you whores, you sell the lives and the memories of your men, you should all be down like stones by the river, you should all be tearing your clothes by the river, the sun and the moon and the wind should stop till you bury the dead, I will, I'll find where they burned the corpse of my father and I'll gather his ashes and the earth that they scorched and I'll carry it to his grave on the hill, you'll see that I will, every ash, every splinter, you'll see that I will, and then maybe you'll stop, and then maybe you'll see: This was my father, and where is Miguel, and this was my father, and where's Emiliano, tell me, tell me, where is your husband, and this was my father, and where is Alonso, Yanina, tell me, Alonso, Antonio, where's Theo, where's Luis, where's Raul, Pablo, Hernando, Claudio, Joaquin, where is Juan, Enrique, Luis, Rafael, Pablo, Armando, Benito, Felipe, Sebastian, Theo, Joaquin, Miguel, Miguel, Miguel, Emiliano, Alonso, Diego, Flaco, where are you, Federico, Ricardo, Eduardo, Saul, Andres, Carlos, Lorenzo, Gabriel, Cristian, where's Segundo, David, Julio, where's Felipe, Angel, Miguel, Roberto, Mario, Ernesto, Salvador, Ernesto . . .

She continues to repeat the names, over and over.

THE WOMEN (*as* SOFIA *lists the names*). Not the names, stop, not the names they'll hear you, they'll hear, no names, no more, no more, not one more name, they can hear, they can hear don't say the names, don't say it, don't say it, don't say . . .

They chant this over and over as ALEXANDRA *says:*

ALEXANDRA (*as* SOFIA *and then the* WOMEN *chant the names*). Get the grain, get the grain, we're going to the market, Fidelia, get the sack, Alexis, the cart, Yani, get the baby, close up the pen, don't listen don't listen, just get the sack and the cart and . . . YOU CRAZY OLD WITCH YOU GIVE THEM NAMES, YOU GO TO THEM AND YOU TELL THEM NAMES, FUENTES, FUENTES, MENDEZ, YOU GIVE THEM OUR NAMES, YOU CALL ATTENTION, YOU'LL KILL THEM ALL, YOU'LL KILL THEM ALL, don't you understand old woman they've got our men . . .

Little pause.

My husband is not dead! Emiliano is not dead. No!

FIDELIA *is picking up the sack during this; the seam gives and the grain spills all over the stage. There is total silence. Everything stops. Everyone looks at the spilled grain.*

ALEXANDRA, *and then the others, including the* WOMEN *from the valley, go down on their hands and knees and start gathering the grain, every kernel. They work in silence.* SOFIA *watches them, and then joins in.*

One of the WOMEN *begins to sob. No one acknowledges this,
and even the sobbing woman doesn't pause in her work. But*
SOFIA *stands slowly, painfully. She lets the handful of grain
she's gathered fall to the ground. She walks to the sobbing
woman, puts her hand on her head. The woman's crying
softens.* SOFIA *leaves. The* WOMEN *work. We hear the sound
of the river, building in volume, becoming menacing.*

Scene 12

*It is dark night. We hear the sound of the river, louder now than
ever. We see a* FIGURE *in the darkness, struggling with something. The* FIGURE *drags a heavy burden from the river and then
sits heavily, clutching it tightly to her. There is a pause, the sound
of the river and the night. Then someone else enters. A match is
struck;* FIDELIA *is standing, holding the match and a candle. She
lights the candle, approaches the figure on the ground. In the
candlelight we see:* SOFIA *sitting, wet, holding a different body.*
FIDELIA *kneels beside her. She blows out the candle. They sit in
the dark.*

Scene 13

*Headlights of a jeep sweeping first the auditorium, then the stage
as though the vehicle was rounding a hill and coming to a stop.
The headlights catch* SOFIA, *clutching the body.* FIDELIA *stands,
backs away.*

LIEUTENANT (*offstage*). There! There! It's . . . Who the fuck . . .
Who the fuck is . . .

(*Giving orders.*) Go around that side, that side, cover the right,
GO!

He enters, behind him soldiers, SOFIA *clutches the body tighter.*

Nobody move, nobody move! Get away from that . . .

ALEXANDRA *enters from the other side.*

ALEXANDRA. Fidelia! Fidelia! Come here, come here, quickly . . .
Sofia.

*A second set of headlights pulls in from the opposite direction,
tyres on gravel coming to a halt. The* CAPTAIN *enters, behind
him* EMMANUEL.

CAPTAIN. What the . . . What is going on here, what is . . .

LIEUTENANT. Get away from that, you old cunt.

CAPTAIN. What's she got, Mrs. Fuentes, what are you . . . Oh my God.

LIEUTENANT. I said get away from that you disgusting old cunt.

He takes his gun out of his holster.

CAPTAIN. Lieutenant. Lieutenant. Put that away.

The LIEUTENANT *doesn't seem to hear the* CAPTAIN.
He cocks the gun. ALEXANDRA *steps in between the*
LIEUTENANT *and* SOFIA. *Other* WOMEN *enter, stand at a*
distance watching.

YANINA. Don't shoot her, don't.

ALEXANDRA. She's just an old woman, there are witnesses, don't . . .

CAPTAIN. Lieutenant, put the gun down and get back in the jeep.

The CAPTAIN *pushes* ALEXANDRA *aside and stands*
between the LIEUTENANT *and the* OLD WOMAN.

CAPTAIN. I am giving you an order. Get back in the jeep.

The LIEUTENANT *hesitates, lowers his gun, turns and leaves.*

CAPTAIN (*to the* WOMEN). Go home. There's nothing here. Go home.

No one moves. He turns to the OLD WOMAN.

CAPTAIN. Mrs. Fuentes. Mrs. Fuentes. Get away from the body.

Where did you . . . Did you find it in the . . . Mrs. Fuentes?

Mrs. Fuentes, will you put that down so we can take a look and see if . . .

SOFIA (*not looking up*). Alexandra?

ALEXANDRA. What, Sofia?

SOFIA. Miguel . . .

CAPTAIN. What did she . . .

ALEXANDRA. She said . . . She thinks it's her husband. She thinks . . .

SOFIA. Miguel.

Pause.

CAPTAIN (*to* ALEXANDRA). Listen. We'll take the body and . . .

SOFIA. NO.

CAPTAIN. I will personally take responsibility for this body. There will be an official . . . We are as concerned about this as . . .

SOFIA. You. Listen to me.

You will have to kill me. Do you understand. You'll have to kill me first.

CAPTAIN (*looks around him at the* WOMEN). I understand.

Do you. Do you want help . . .

SOFIA. No help.

ALEXANDRA. We'll carry him. Sofia. Sofia, come.

The other WOMEN *approach. Together they all pick up the body, heavy with river water. They carry it past the* SOLDIERS *and out.*

CAPTAIN. TWO fucking bodies! TWO! Someone is setting me up, I . . .

Tell the Lieutenant to get his butt over here. Now.

EMMANUEL *exits.*

CAPTAIN. Stink-hole. Fucking stink-hole. Plug the goddamed river up. Make a . . . a lake. With a concrete bottom. Clean. Paddle-boats on Sundays. That's better. That's it.

The LIEUTENANT *enters,* EMMANUEL *behind. The* LIEUTENANT *and the* CAPTAIN *glare at each other. The* CAPTAIN *makes* EMMANUEL *leave.*

LIEUTENANT. Where do you think these bodies are coming from?

CAPTAIN. Where do you think they're coming from?

LIEUTENANT. I asked you first.

CAPTAIN. I'm your superior.

LIEUTENANT. Then you must be smarter than me.

CAPTAIN. I am.

LIEUTENANT. Then answer my question. Sir.

CAPTAIN. I think someone wants to make trouble for me.

LIEUTENANT. I think someone wants to make trouble for me.

CAPTAIN. Who? Why would anyone want to do that? You're such a charming young man.

LIEUTENANT. But some people, I think, are immune to my charms.

The Communists. The Terrorists. The Subversives. That old woman. She's doing it! They're tossing these bodies in, using you to get rid of people like me, people who are effective. If Fuentes is buried, then she'll ask who killed him, and then they ask who arrested him, and then they trace a trail back to me.

CAPTAIN. Paranoid bullshit. You're doing it! You and your effective friends! You throw the bodies in the river so she can find them and she gets wild and I am expected to abandon my programme and start shooting . . .

LIEUTENANT. Oh, shooting! You're so delicate, captain. This, this reform, this delicacy, it will end with me on trial. And you on trial too, for what you did somewhere else, can't you see that?

CAPTAIN. There'll be no trials. Trials come when bodies float downstream. So in case you happen to know who's throwing them in . . .

LIEUTENANT. I DON'T KNOW WHO . . .

CAPTAIN (*overlapping*). Tell them to be smart, ask themselves what their best interests really are, because at this moment – it's in my best interest to point my guns not at these women but at . . . anyone I see getting in my way.

Little pause.

LIEUTENANT. I thank you for your friendly, middle-class advice. And here's some for you.

Everything we do here is being watched. By important people. The true defenders of the motherland.

So if the funeral happens, an hour later you'll get a phone call announcing your demotion. And a day or two later you'll find yourself back in the capital where the streets are crowded and cars speed by and one speeding past you some morning has a man inside with a gun and a bullet.

CAPTAIN. Save your threats, you . . .

LIEUTENANT. And back here in the valley of hell the guns will be pointed at our enemies again.

You betrayed me. You sided with that crow. All of those women saw that.

CAPTAIN. Lieutenant . . .

LIEUTENANT. I mean it, Captain. Don't let her bury that body.

The LIEUTENANT *nods, leaves.*

On another side of the stage, the FUENTES *family enters with the body. Silently washes it and prepares it for burial.*

CAPTAIN (*apparently alone*). Damn.

You were listening the whole time?

Emmanuel?

EMMANUEL *appears.*

CAPTAIN. My little shadow. I wish you wouldn't do that.

I think . . . I may have gone too far.

EMMANUEL. The Lieutenant seemed upset.

CAPTAIN. How observant.

EMMANUEL. May I make a suggestion? Captain?

CAPTAIN. Oh please do. You're so thoroughly informed, after all.

EMMANUEL. You didn't know Miguel Fuentes. Maybe you made a mistake.

CAPTAIN. A mistake.

EMMANUEL. If someone else claimed the body, a competing claim. Maybe it was someone else's husband. Someone whose husband died accidentally. There are men missing the Lieutenant didn't arrest, whose funerals wouldn't worry the Lieutenant.

CAPTAIN. Got anyone in mind?

EMMANUEL. Theo Sanjines.

CAPTAIN. Someone you . . .

EMMANUEL. I know his wife. . . Cecilia Sanjines. My girlfriend. Now she is.

CAPTAIN. Urqueta was right. You're a credit to your kind.

You eavesdrop on my conversations. You probably open my mail. Whose ears are you? Who do you listen for? Kastoria?

Little pause.

EMMANUEL. With your permission, Captain, but I want to leave this place. So does Cecilia. And Philip Kastoria doesn't seem to think that's such a good idea.

CAPTAIN. Does Kastoria know about the bodies?

EMMANUEL. Mr. Kastoria used to say, sir: 'Not a leaf falls on my land without me knowing it.'

CAPTAIN. The Kastorias must be close to the Lieutenant. The Families.

EMMANUEL. There are luncheons, sir, the Lieutenant is invited.

CAPTAIN. Uh huh.

If you happen to find yourself upriver again, it would be in your interests to give Mr. Kastoria the impression . . . that I am in control. Because, Orderly, if I succeed here I will be very grateful to those who help me.

Now. I think our co-operative widow. . .

EMMANUEL. Mrs. Sanjines.

CAPTAIN. Should be informed that her husband has drowned. A most unpleasant task. I'm sure you'll find a way of comforting her.

EMMANUEL. Yes sir. . . And what about . . . the old woman, sir?

CAPTAIN (*he sits at the river bank in Sofia's spot*). If I sit like her, will a body come to me?

Where, where where are the bodies coming from?

Little pause.

That old woman's grandson. How old?

EMMANUEL. Um, thirteen, fourteen, I . . .

CAPTAIN (*standing*). A little detour through the shit. To the future. God willing.

Scene 14

CECILIA *and* EMMANUEL.

EMMANUEL. You want him to come back.

CECILIA. I want you.

EMMANUEL. Then bury him.

CECILIA. But that's not him.

EMMANUEL. It is if you say so.

CECILIA. No. It's someone else. Theo will come back .

EMMANUEL. Bury him and he won't.

CECILIA. I wish it was that simple.

EMMANUEL. It is. Listen to me: bury him and he'll never come back. You do this for the Captain and the Captain will make certain Theo never shows up again.

Little pause.

CECILIA. I can't do that.

EMMANUEL. Choose. Him or me.

Little pause, then CECILIA *kisses* EMMANUEL.

CECILIA. Promise me: when we get to the city we'll have thousands of children.

EMMANUEL. Millions, not thousands, millions.

CECILIA. And every one of them with your eyes.

Scene 15

The FUENTES *family gathered in a room around the body, washed and dressed now and laid out on a rough bier. Red sunrise, candles.*

SOFIA. When I was just a girl, my sisters and I went to town, dressed in bright dresses our grandma made, for the festival of the planting. You could see the torches in the square from afar off, all the way up the mountain, and we rode down in a cart . . . It was so late when we got to the square, and my sisters, may they rest in peace, they vanished right away, into the crowd, all those tall farmers . . . and there was music and then I felt his hands on my shoulders, behind me. He said don't turn around, and he took my red scarf and covered my eyes, and tied it behind me, so all I could see when I opened my eyes was bright red. And he led me blind to the dance.

FIDELIA. Then what?

SOFIA. I've told you so often what happened next. We danced. I couldn't see him. I felt him. He was only a boy, but I was only a girl, and the band started playing something, a song with a strange rhythm I didn't know, and I said to him take off this scarf, you idiot, I can't see and I don't know how to do this dance, and he said leave it on I'll teach you, and I said why

should you see when I can't? And he said he couldn't see
either, his eyes were closed. And I thought that was funny so
I let him dance with me even though I thought probably he's
crazy. Miguel. And after the dance was over he took off the
scarf and looked at me and said Oh! You're beautiful.

FIDELIA. Were you?

SOFIA. No, I was ugly. But that's what he said.

I could always recognize him, from that night on, even with my
eyes closed, even blind, in the dark. I could always recognize
my Miguel.

Scene 16

FATHER GABRIEL *and the* CAPTAIN.

CAPTAIN. I'm troubled.

You've heard about the body in the river. It can't be properly
identified. But a widow claims it as the body of her man. So
I've taken a risk. It seemed, well . . .

FATHER GABRIEL. Compassionate.

CAPTAIN. Yes. To let her have the body to bury.

Have I sinned in allowing her this funeral, even though I have
my doubts that the corpse is hers?

FATHER GABRIEL. I've asked myself the same question,
Captain.

CAPTAIN. Yes.

FATHER GABRIEL. After all, I have to perform the rites, and . . .

CAPTAIN. Since you aren't certain . . .

FATHER GABRIEL. I've seen the body. I have serious doubts.

CAPTAIN. But?

FATHER GABRIEL. These are troubled times. These women
need an end to the uncertainty, the not-knowing is . . .
intolerable. It's a peculiar form of Hell.

If a burial can bring peace, then in the name of a greater good
I would perform the funeral.

CAPTAIN. And trust that the Heavenly Father will forgive.

FATHER GABRIEL. Since we act in the name of peace, yes.

CAPTAIN. I can't tell you how much this relieves me, Father.

FATHER GABRIEL. And it will relieve the torment of Sofia
    Fuentes.

CAPTAIN. Sofia Fuentes. Ah, then you haven't heard.

    That was . . . a mistake. Mrs. Fuentes was mistaken. The body
    has been claimed by Cecilia Sanjines.

FATHER GABRIEL. Cecilia?

CAPTAIN. Her husband, Theo Sanjines. Missing for seven
    months. Apparently a heavy drinker, he . . . used to beat his
    wife. A lot of these men did.

    Odd that she hasn't contacted you about the service. No doubt
    she's still in shock.

    Little pause.

FATHER GABRIEL. Captain, I can't . . . You gave that body to
    Sofia Fuentes.

CAPTAIN. But you yourself said it didn't look like . . .

FATHER GABRIEL. It was unrecognizable. Why is one woman's
    claim better than another's?

CAPTAIN. In this affair I have had to play Solomon. I can't cut
    the corpse in two, can I? So the widow whose claim seems
    most probable gets the body.

    Little pause.

FATHER GABRIEL. I won't do it. I can't. Miguel Fuentes was
    my friend. He sat in the chair you're sitting in, many nights,
    he . . .

CAPTAIN. Then you'll want to help his family.

FATHER GABRIEL. They won't consider it a help to . . .

CAPTAIN. But they will. You see, in exchange for your pastoral
    assistance in the funeral of Theo Sanjines, and in exchange for
    the good-natured co-operation of the Fuentes family, I would
    be prepared to release a prisoner, a relative of theirs.

FATHER GABRIEL. Emiliano? Alonso?

CAPTAIN. Um, I think his name is Alexis.

FATHER GABRIEL. No, Alexis is the boy.

CAPTAIN. Yes. Him.

Pause.

FATHER GABRIEL. He isn't . . .

CAPTAIN. We arrested him this afternoon.

Little pause.

FATHER GABRIEL. Please. . . please don't hurt the boy.

CAPTAIN. I will tell Mrs. Sanjines to expect your call. Be careful with her, she's very upset.

Hurt the boy?

I know what you think of me, Father.

FATHER GABRIEL. I don't think you do.

CAPTAIN. I can imagine. Don't judge me. I am . . . It sickens me, I hate pain, terror, but at times I'm forced to . . . We have to follow our hearts to the greater good. There are forces at work here – who intend nothing good for this country. I intend peace. I want that as much as you. But sometimes the road to peace is, as you know, fraught with difficult choices. You shouldn't judge me too hastily.

FATHER GABRIEL. I don't, Captain. The dead will judge the dead.

Little pause. The CAPTAIN *kneels.*

CAPTAIN. Bless me Father. For I have sinned.

Lights go down on CAPTAIN *and* FATHER GABRIEL. *Only a light on the chair where the* CAPTAIN *sat remains. From the shadows, the* NARRATOR *emerges, goes to the chair.*

Scene 17

NARRATOR. As for me, I am not so different from the interpreters in their glass booths at endless international conferences on torture, not so different from them with their monochrome voices their dictionaries their notes their culture their going back home in Geneva in New York in the Hague, an intermediary, not even a bridge, simultaneous translation for good pay, a specialist in language rather than suffering.

They listen, they jot down, they find the right adjective.

Like them, I must watch from afar what I cannot remedy.

Like them, I cannot speak to those whom I translate, I cannot give them advice, I cannot even tell those I am hearing to watch out.

And like the interpreters, I am not in danger. It is true that if I had stayed in my country, it would be my words that someone faraway would be struggling to put into a perfect foreign language, struggling to bury in another language.

But now that the years of exile pass and pass, now that I cannot remember the colour of the eyes of my children, I am becoming more and more like the intepreters.

With this difference.

Unlike them, I cannot switch off the voices.

Unlike them, I am haunted by those voices.

Unlike them, I cannot stop listening.

The lights change, diminishing but not disappearing on the NARRATOR, *remaining very strongly on the chair in the darkness. Another, stranger, light comes up on* FIDELIA. *She looks towards the chair.*

FIDELIA. Are you in pain? Are you in pain? Can I do . . . something to help you? Are you in pain?

THE WOMEN (*as lights raise on them*). Yes, he is in pain, yes, Fidelia, he is.

The lights begin to fade on the empty chair and rise on the chair next to it. Seated in this chair is a naked MAN, *breathing heavily, with a black cloth hood over his head. He hardly moves. It is difficult to tell from his body how old he is, but he's very thin.*

FIDELIA. What can I do for him, how can I help him, can I go to where he is?

THE WOMEN. No, Fidelia, you can't do that, the door is locked, it's too far.

FIDELIA. Can I give him water, is he thirsty, medicine, is he hurt, what can I . . . ?

THE WOMEN. Talk to him, girl, he can hear you, talk to him, tell him a story.

FIDELIA. A story? A story, I don't . . . What kind of story, a story about what?

THE WOMEN. About this, Fidelia, the story of what happened.

DELIA. Not that, that will hurt him, I don't want to tell him that, I can't, I can't . . .

THE WOMEN. The truth, Fidelia, the story of what happened.

FIDELIA. I don't know how.

I saw a bird, a dead bird, on its back, its throat was pulled back, like this, its beak was open, it was trying to . . . to fly, no, it was . . . trying to drink . . . it was drinking in light, it was trying to do that. No, that's not . . .

The door. They kicked in the door, they splintered, the door, Mama screamed, she screamed . . . about the bird, no, she . . . screamed . . . something, it was . . . 'Take me', she said, I think she . . . but then, but then, but they knew, he was down in the corn down in the corn, he was hid in the corn but they knew, who told them, and she screamed, and she screamed, but they went through the fields, like fire, so fast, and they trampled the corn, and they picked him, like a plant, they tore at the roots, they picked him out from the corn, and she kept on screaming but making no sounds, and . . .

And where was I, when they took my . . . where was I standing, I was standing by mama, no, I was . . . not, I was out in the corn, I was . . . up in the air I was . . . flying above it and . . . no, I was . . . dead I was . . . lying on my back, trying . . . to drink in the light but . . . I don't know how to tell you this story, papa, I don't know what story I'm trying to tell, I . . .

Papa? Are you there?

They took him, papa. They took Alexis away.

Scene 18

The cemetery on the hill; generations upon generations of plain peasant graves.

CECILIA, EMMANUEL, *the* CAPTAIN *and the* LIEUTENANT *by a freshly-dug grave. They are waiting for the* FUENTES *family to deliver the body.* FATHER GABRIEL *stands apart. No one says anything.* ALEXANDRA, YANINA *and* SOFIA *arrive with the corpse.*

ALEXANDRA. Where's my son?

CAPTAIN. Lieutenant, the boy.

The LIEUTENANT *exits. Silence.*

CAPTAIN (*to the Fuentes women*). I assume you know Mrs. Sanjines.

Silence.

Mrs. Sanjines, you know . . .

CECILIA (*barely audible*). Yes.

Alexandra, I'm sorry.

ALEXANDRA. Theo will kill you.

ALEXANDRA *turns her back on* CECILIA.

CAPTAIN. Ladies, please.

The LIEUTENANT *re-enters with* ALEXIS. *The boy is unsteady on his feet, his shirt has been torn and hastily repatched, he looks at the ground and keeps one eye closed. From the other side of the stage,* FIDELIA *appears with the* BABY. *She watches the scene from afar.*

CAPTAIN (*thrown by the appearance of* ALEXIS). Um . . . Good. Good . . . now we can . . .

ALEXANDRA *walks to the* LIEUTENANT *and* ALEXIS, *she takes* ALEXIS *by the arm, he cries out, pulls away.* ALEXANDRA *turns to the* CAPTAIN.

ALEXANDRA. What did . . . what did you . . . ?

LIEUTENANT. He's alive. Be thankful. Next time, save us the trouble.

Captain, your prisoner.

The LIEUTENANT *exits.*

CAPTAIN (*rattled*). Suspected subversives will be interrogated according to official procedures.

Don't misunderstand me. I am as committed as ever to peace but . . . I cannot permit subversion of my authority.

Mrs. Fuentes, Thank you for returning the body of Mr. Sanjines. We apologize for the grotesque mistake. Now take your grandson and go home.

Mrs. Fuentes.

Mrs. Fuentes.

He goes to ALEXIS, *grabs his arm.* ALEXIS *cries out.*

Woman, you haven't begun to see the trouble I can cause.

ALEXANDRA. Sofia . . .

> SOFIA *strengthens her grip on the body. No one moves. Then she lets go, turns, goes to her grandson, puts an arm gingerly around him and leads him away from the* CAPTAIN.

> *The* CAPTAIN *signals to the two* SOLDIERS. *They move to the cart. They pick up the corpse and carry it to the grave. They place it in the pit.*

CAPTAIN. Mrs. Sanjines . . .

> EMMANUEL *nudges* CECILIA, *who stumbles a little and then walks quickly to the grave. Not looking in, she pitches a flower at the corpse and turns and almost exits.* EMMANUEL *stops her.*

CAPTAIN. Father . . .

FATHER GABRIEL. Father in Heaven, here is . . . one of Your children. We . . .

CAPTAIN. Name.

FATHER GABRIEL. Theo Sanjines. Father, show mercy for my friend Theo Sanjines. Wherever his soul may be.

> Ashes to ashes, earth to earth, dust you were and dust you are and to dust you shall return. Amen.

> *Little pause.*

CAPTAIN. Thank you. Mrs. Sanjines, my condolences.

> CECILIA *exits quickly.* EMMANUEL *follows her.*

CAPTAIN (*to* ALEXANDRA). The army will reimburse you for the cost of the shroud.

> Good day.

> *The* CAPTAIN *exits. The two* SOLDIERS *hastily fill in the grave.*

FATHER GABRIEL. Sofia. God works in strange ways. Maybe this is a sign – that he – that Miguel is alive. You should never give up hope.

> *Little pause.*

> Please forgive me. All of you.

> *Exits.*

> *The* SOLDIERS *hammer a flimsy wooden cross into the earth at the head of the grave, and exit.*

ALEXANDRA. Sofia. Thank you.

SOFIA. Miguel. Is so ashamed of me.

She exits.

ALEXANDRA. Alexis.

ALEXANDRA *goes to* ALEXIS. *She leads him off, followed by* YANINA. FIDELIA *stays behind, always at a distance from the tombs, as if she inhabited a separate dimension. She speaks to the child.*

FIDELIA. Say something. Say 'Ma.' Every baby your age can say 'Ma'.

She looks at the audience.

Maybe he won't ever say anything. Maybe he'll just be quiet. And never tell a story to anybody. Until the day he dies.

She exits with the baby.

Scene 19

We watch night fall on the graveyard, and then fade as a dawn light grows and builds: The graveyard, the next morning, a beautiful day. SOFIA *enters, hair unplaited and wild. She is carrying bread, which she places on* THEO's *grave. She looks at the mound. She takes clumps of the earth in her hands and examines them. She holds it to her face, and inhales deeply. Then she rubs some of it across her chest, sensually, between her legs, and then crumbles the remaining earth to the ground. She picks up the loaf of bread, tears it in half, and puts one half back on the ground. She is biting into her half when the first woman enters; she too is carrying bread. Other* WOMEN *arrive; each, one at a time, tears her loaf in half and leaves it on* THEO's *grave, till soon the grave is a mound of freshly-baked loaves.* YANINA *goes to sit by* SOFIA *at the grave;* ALEXANDRA *has come too but sits apart. The women sit around it, eating.*

KATHERINA. I knew when I saw the first body come out of the river, the minute I laid hands on him I knew it was my brother. I should have insisted. I was afraid.

TERESA. It wasn't your brother. It was my nephew. I recognized him. I was too afraid to speak. When you said to the lieutenant that you thought you recognized your brother, I thought to myself, she's crazy, she's wrong but at least she has the courage to speak.

ROSA. The first body, well I can't be absolutely certain but the hands, even broken, I think it was Luisa's oldest son. I am absolutely sure that the second body, though, was . . .

TERESA. That was my husband. No doubt about that.

MARILUZ. My father.

ROSA. My father. I baked all night. This is my father in this grave. I baked bread for his grave.

TERESA. This is very confusing.

AMANDA. Everyone baked. All night. The whole valley smelled of yeast rising.

TERESA. So does everyone think . . . ?

KATHERINA. Maybe it isn't anyone's. Maybe everyone's wrong.

MARILUZ. Maybe everyone's right.

TERESA. Impossible. It can't belong to all of us. It's only one body.

KATHERINA. Yes. And it's my son, Eduardo.

TERESA. It's Antonio. It's my husband. He was that thin.

ROSA. It's my father.

MARILUZ. No, mine. Ernesto Torres. I'd stake my life on it.

AMANDA. It didn't look a thing like your father, he wasn't nearly so tall, it was . . .

·LUCIA. It was Cesar. That pig. He beat me, I hated him, I was going to leave the bastard, but then they took him. As long as I didn't know if he was alive or dead I was stuck with him forever. Now I can . . .

TERESA. You can what?

LUCIA. Dig up the little shit, bury him proper, and then dance on his grave.

Some of the women laugh, KATHERINA *hushes them.*

TERESA. But it's only one body. And everyone wants to bury it.

What are we going to do about that?

SOFIA. You know what to do. You told me how to do it.

Go get permission. And then bury your men.

TERESA. But it's just this one poor . . .

SOFIA. That's not our problem. You identify? Then you must bury. Ask permission. Let the captain figure it out.

The WOMEN *start to stand. The cry of a bird, overhead. Then the lights begin to change. There is the sound of the river, and a sense of rushing water, and something magical. One of the women speaks first, and the others join in under her, perhaps singing, or chanting, or repeating her incantation.*

THE WOMEN. The water knows, the water has been there, the water is curious, it wants to find out, it will flood in your ears, in your eyes, in your mouth it will carry out the words, from the deepest places, the memories the pain, it will carry your stories over miles of river, calling the stories as it moves to the sea, it will sing to the valleys with a stoney voice, the water the throat drinks, the rain that he sees the mud that he walks in the soup that they eat the sweat that falls and the other water the other water and some rivers are wide, and calm, green and smooth, and some are sharp and high, they fall clear from the mountains, and ours is a river that is shallow, cold and brown, and it brings us our men, over miles of stone beds, it tumbles them home, but there are so many men who are missing or dead, so many the river cannot carry them all, too many stories for the river to tell too many stories so it brought us back one, and the godless they burnt it, and it brought us another, to bury on the hill, and it tumbled the body, over and over, till all of its features were murmured away . . . because if the river carried all the men home, their bodies would dam it, they would strangle the river, and the valley would flood, and the field turn to swamp, where nothing can grow, and everything rots, and it found us this body, and it made it any body, and it made it every body, and it's mine, it's mine, oh please don't let it be mine, it's mine, oh please don't let it be mine, it's mine, oh please, oh please, oh please, oh please . . .

The WOMEN *then each in turn individually say: 'It's mine.'*

End of Act Two.

ACT THREE

Scene 20

The CAPTAIN *and* EMMANUEL; *the* WIDOWS *queued up.*
TERESA SALAS *in a chair.*

CAPTAIN. Thirty-six widows! What the fuck am I supposed to do
with thirty-six widows! Widows, mothers, aunts, grandmas –
the only woman in the whole miserable fucking valley who
isn't demanding that corpse is the one woman we gave it to!
And where the fuck is she, Orderly?

EMMANUEL. I can't find her, Captain, I don't know . . .

CAPTAIN. You seem to know a whole fuck of a lot less than I
thought you did, this whole mess, well, I'd say it was all your
fault if you were important enough to matter, but you don't,
you're just my little peasant orderly who tries too hard to be
helpful and I let myself forget, no progress without order, but
now I'm taking control.

Your girlfriend's the official widow in this hideous mess and if
you want me to transfer you out of here you'd better find her.

EMMANUEL *salutes and exits.*

CAPTAIN. Someone's set me up, someone's making a joke of me,
the press will hear about this and then . . . We don't do well in
sports or beauty contests. Finally we have a record to be proud
of: More widows per corpse than any other country in the
world.

TERESA. My name is Teresa Salas, I am 53 years old, my husband
Antonio Salas, he would have been 59 years old last March, he
was mayor of Camacho. He was elected when we last had an
election; when we stopped having elections, he was arrested for
trying to reclaim the land. And taken away on February 20th
eight years ago and I never saw him again. Until two days ago
when . . . when his body washed up in the river. And now
I want to bury him. In the cemetery by his parents' graves.

CAPTAIN (*flipping through a stack of claims*). Husband brother
husband father son nephew son son . . . lover . . . husband
husband uncle husband . . .

So which woman's claim is . . .

I mean it can't belong to all of you. It's only one body.

TERESA. My husband's.

CAPTAIN. So the other women are wrong.

Pause.

Right? One of you is right and the other thirty-six have to be mistaken. Right?

TERESA. It's not my job to explain. I know what I know. They know what they know. I know it is my husband.

CAPTAIN. You don't know you don't know that's the point, none of you knows anything, you're all mentally underdeveloped emotionally overdeveloped superstitious mindless peasants and this . . . preposterous little scandal you've cooked up – you have no idea the trouble this is causing, you have no idea . . . what you're spoiling here with this demented, backwards . . .

TERESA (*pulling a locket from her blouse, moving with startling energy and abruptness to the Captain, speaking vehemently*). Backwards? Is it backwards to want to bury your dead? Don't you want your wife to do it for you? This is my husband who I lived with for thirty-two years – no, don't look away.

She tears the locket from her neck, slams it on the desk.

This is my husband I slept with every night for thirty-two years, what do you mean how do I know? What do you mean backwards? I know.

CAPTAIN (*quietly, picking up the locket*). Enough, Mrs. Salas.

TERESA. They shot my sixteen-year-old son in the back of his head. I . . . saw . . . that. They . . . did . . . that.

CAPTAIN (*still quiet*). I said that's enough.

TERESA. If this is not my husband, then where is he? If this is not his body, then give him to me alive. If you won't do that, then let me bury him.

Pause.

CAPTAIN. You want to bury this body that you say is your husband. But what if your husband . . . walked through that door now? What if I clap my hands, like this: (*He claps.*) and he walked through the door.

The door begins to open; TERESA spins around towards it. The LIEUTENANT enters. TERESA stares at him then looks away.

CAPTAIN. What would you do if your husband came through that door?

TERESA. I would thank you, Captain. If he came back alive. What else could I do?

CAPTAIN. Yes.

That's all, Mrs. Salas.

I said that's all.

Tell the next widow I'm going to lunch.

She exits.

CAPTAIN. I didn't call for you.

LIEUTENANT. I wanted to gloat.

CAPTAIN. Gloat somewhere else. I'm busy. There are seventeen other . . .

LIEUTENANT. This is more fun than a circus. The Captain and his amazing multiplying widows. What's your next trick?

CAPTAIN. A surprise.

LIEUTENANT. Take control here. That'd surprise everyone.

CAPTAIN. I'll tell you a story.

My father had a dog, and he beat it every day.

LIEUTENANT. Captain, I really don't want to . . .

CAPTAIN. Sit down and shut the fuck up and listen to my story, Lieutenant. That's an order.

My father had this dog . . .

LIEUTENANT. And he beat it every day.

CAPTAIN. Right. Then one day, without warning, it bit him. Locked onto him. I was alone with him in the house. He sent me for his pistol – he was a Colonel – he told me how to load it, all this with the dog eating up his arm, screaming at me, my father – and when it was loaded, I shot the dog. And it still wouldn't let go. It had finally gotten what it wanted after all those years of beatings and even after death it wasn't going to let go. So I had to get his hunting knife and begin to work on its teeth. I was seven years old.

LIEUTENANT. That's . . . illuminating. A parable. You shot the dog.

CAPTAIN. Had to.

LIEUTENANT. Will you shoot here?

CAPTAIN. Ah, but you miss the parable's point. You're too easily distracted by guns.

LIEUTENANT. So what's the point?

CAPTAIN. The point is: When you back people against the wall, they may surrender. Or they may put up a fight that will leave you crippled. My father was never able to use that arm again in his life.

People get hurt. That's the point.

LIEUTENANT. These people are used to being beaten. The point here is: make sure they don't forget who's holding the leash. If you are holding the leash.

At least you've got me to command. You're my captain, Captain. Bow wow.

CAPTAIN. I'll tell you something: There's a part of me that would love to shoot one or two of those women. There's a part of me that would love to shoot you.

But any thug can use a gun. They can make trouble and you can make threats, but we have to move ahead, and we'll drag the rest of you kicking and screaming into the twentieth century.

LIEUTENANT. The twentieth century? We're already there.

CAPTAIN. Not in this country we're not.

LIEUTENANT. On the contrary. What would the twentieth century be without countries like ours?

So what bone will you throw them?

CAPTAIN. Now that's the real surprise.

Scene 21

NARRATOR. I like to tell myself that this is my revenge. I like to tell myself that if I had not been expelled from my country, this story would not have been told.

After all, I made it up, word for word, character by character, all invented while I watched from afar my country resisting and then being raped, the legs of each object of my country being forced open, the arms of each object in my country being pinned down so the legs could be forced open, every last thing in my country eroded and made unfamiliar, filled with the wrong seed, I wrote it all down night after night after night because there was nothing else I could with myself, no other way to keep hope alive.

And yet, I am beginning to suspect that rather than the creator of this story, I am becoming its parasite, a tourist of horror, the voyeur of a struggle I could not join – possessed by peasant women I know nothing about, lives I had barely glanced at from a passing car, people I had no right to speak for.

I feel more and more that I am the mirror of a mirror and that they are the ones who invented me, whispered life to me in the dark, imagined someone like me to carry their story, so I could tell it to those remote people who spend their lives indifferently switching indifferent channels, those supposedly safe people who need to know even if they are not aware of their need.

Who is to say that I am not the invention of those women? Are you sure, as you sit there, like me, watching them, that you have more – let me say the word – more reality than they do?

Are you sure that someone has not invented you?

Who are we to say that this story did not happen, that it is not happening somewhere at this very moment?

Scene 22

EMMANUEL *and* CECILIA *at the river; she's got a suitcase and she's dishevelled, clambering along the riverbank with* EMMANUEL *in pursuit.*

EMMANUEL. You're fucking everything up, please, baby, you have to . . .

CECILIA. I have to get away from here. You lied. You said he wasn't coming back, but he is, he'll see the grave, they'll tell him what I . . .

EMMANUEL. He's dead. Theo is dead.

CECILIA. He's not.

EMMANUEL. I killed him.

CECILIA. You're a liar.

EMMANUEL. You don't want him dead. You don't love me.

CECILIA. Take me to the city. Now. Then I'll be better. Then I can forget, I can't here, but there . . . We have to go now, we . . .

She stops suddenly, looking ahead of her at the river.

CECILIA. Oh no, oh no . . .

EMMANUEL. What? What is it? Celia?

In a terrible panic CELIA *begins running away from the river. He stands, pulling his gun out, looking where she's looked. He sees nothing, he runs after her, grabs her.*

CECILIA (*wild with terror*). Let me go, let me . . .

EMMANUEL. What's wrong what's wrong, there's nothing . . .

CECILIA. It's him! It's him! In the river, it's . . .

EMMANUEL. There's nothing in the river!

CECILIA. Theo's in the water, I saw . . .

She breaks away and now begins to run towards the river.

EMMANUEL. Stop, Cecilia, goddamn it I said stop!

He fires his gun into the air. She stops but doesn't turn to look at him.

CECILIA. Don't. Please don't kill me.

EMMANUEL *walks past her to the river.*

CECILIA. Oh God forgive me, God forgive me . . .

EMMANUEL. Shut up, shut the fuck up. It's . . .

EMMANUEL *wades into the river. He returns carrying a wet tattered piece of black cloth.*

EMMANUEL. See? Nothing. River trash. See.

Scared the shit out of me. Women . . .

See?

CECILIA. Put the gun away.

EMMANUEL (*putting the gun away*). Did you really think it was . . .

CECILIA. It was. I thought it was. Yes.

EMMANUEL. But it wasn't.

They stand looking at each other, winded.

EMMANUEL. It wasn't. Say it wasn't Theo.

CECILIA. It . . . wasn't him.

EMMANUEL. Say 'Theo's never coming back.'

Pause.

Say 'Theo's never coming back.'

Pause.

I'm leaving.

He starts to exit, she follows, he turns.

EMMANUEL. You stay. By the river. With him.

Just don't . . . Don't come near me again.

CECILIA. I can't be alone. I'll kill myself.

EMMANUEL. I'm going to the city. That's where I belong. I'll find a woman there without dirty hands, a woman who's never washed in a river. Peasant.

CECILIA. I'll kill myself.

EMMANUEL. I hope you all do. It's deep enough here. Do it.

Scene 23

The CAPTAIN *alone on stage. As he speaks the women of the village assemble, except* FIDELIA, *who watches from the other side of the stage with the baby in her arms. Next to her is* ALEXIS.

CAPTAIN. When I arrived here in Camacho I believed . . . we had a bargain. That I would exercise my authority with reason and restraint, and you would learn to look forward to what life could become.

Well I've lived up to my side of the bargain and you haven't lived up to yours.

You have made yourselves a spectacle, with this half-witted conspiracy to mock me, but . . . We are stuck with one another. And I intend to show you that you can forgive your adversaries and even do them a service. In the name of that future life.

I am pleased to release the first prisoner under the terms of the amnesty decree.

You see, whoever it is dumping dead bodies in the river can only give you dead bodies. I can give you living men.

He claps his hands. There is an absolute silence – none of the WOMEN *is breathing. Two* SOLDIERS *come in escorting a* MAN, *who walks stooped and stiff. They lead him to face the* WOMAN. *He never raises his head.*

There is another silence. None of the WOMEN *move. They stare at the* MAN – *maybe they recognize him, or are afraid they do.*

CAPTAIN (*clearing his throat*). Sofia Fuentes. This afternoon. Alonso Fuentes. Your son.

Scene 24

Lights change and everyone leaves, except the FUENTES WOMEN *as the Fuentes' house materializes around them.* YANINA *takes the baby from* FIDELIA.

YANINA. He's coming back, my heavy little man, I promised you he would. He's tall, your papa, like a tree, but don't be scared of him.

ALEXANDRA. We have to hurry, he'll be here soon.

ALEXANDRA *takes the baby from* YANINA *and gives him to* ALEXIS, *who leaves as* SOFIA *enters with the bathing equipment.* YANINA *removes her widow's black. She's naked, although partially hidden from the audience by the women who surround her and bathe her.*

SOFIA. Don't catch cold.

When they're done, SOFIA *takes a blanket and wraps* YANINA *in it. They exit.* ALEXANDRA *and* FIDELIA *are left alone in the yard.*

FIDELIA. Why did they let Alonso go, and not papa?

Pause.

Are you happy for Yani, mama?

ALEXANDRA (*smiling a little*). Oh Fidelia. Why do you always ask such . . . hard questions? Come here.

Mother and daughter stand looking at each other.

ALEXANDRA. Your father too. He asks hard questions. You're both pains in the ass.

When the women were claiming they recognized . . . For a moment I almost wanted it to be him, it would almost be a relief. Do you understand?

FIDELIA. Yes, mama.

ALEXANDRA. You're a smart girl.

I can't tell you how much I hurt.

YANINA *appears in the doorway in a brilliant green dress.* ALEXANDRA *turns around.*

ALEXANDRA (*after a little pause*). Where? Where did you . . .

YANINA. Alonso. When I got pregnant he went into town and bought it for me. He said so he'd remember, when I got big with the baby, what I'd look like after the baby was born. I never wore it, since he . . . went away before. Do . . . Do I look OK?

ALEXANDRA. You look . . . you look like a fancy lady.

YANINA. How fancy?

ALEXANDRA. Ten pesos an hour.

They look at each other and both start to laugh.

YANINA. Oh Alex. Oh Alex I'm so sorry . . .

ALEXANDRA. Shut up.

YANINA. Do I smell OK?

ALEXANDRA. Mmmm. Like pine sap. Mmmm.

YANINA. Like on my wedding night.

ALEXANDRA. On your wedding night you smelled like cheap wine.

ALEXIS *comes into the yard from the house carrying the baby.*

YANINA. Oh I got so drunk . . .

They laugh and embrace. ALONSO *steps into the yard. The women don't see him.* ALEXIS *does. He looks at* ALONSO *for a moment and then says:.*

ALEXIS. Ma . . . ? Mama, he's . . .

YANINA *and* ALEXANDRA *turn. A frozen moment, then* YANINA *runs to* ALONSO *and they embrace.* SOFIA *and* FIDELIA *come out of the house.*

SOFIA. We've made some soup, it will . . .

SOFIA *and* ALONSO *look at each other. Behind him, the other* WOMEN *of the valley drift in.*

YANINA. Sofia? Sofia come here, it's your son, don't you . . .

Look how thin he is, he's so thin, and pale you can see through him almost, Sofia.

SOFIA. It's not him.

YANINA. What are you talking about, of course it is, it's . . .

SOFIA. It's his body but it's not him.

YANINA. Oh she's lost her mind completely, Alexandra, tell her to . . .

SOFIA. Where's his soul? What have they done with his soul? Ask him that.

His soul's with the others. Ask him where they are.

Ask him what he did . . . to make them let his body go?

What did you do, my baby? Who did you have to betray?

YANINA. Oh God she . . . Sofia, stop. This is Alonso, this is your son, he . . .

He never had anything to do with that, with politics, what could he have done, betray, he didn't know anything, Alonso, tell her, tell her you don't know what she's talking about, tell her . . .

She goes to ALEXIS, *takes the baby from him.*

YANINA. Look, this is your son, this is . . .

ALONSO. I . . . Yes. I . . .

YANINA. Come inside, come inside, don't you want to . . .

ALONSO *kneels slowly. He lowers his head.*

ALONSO. They keep you blindfolded in a room. You know where they're taking you by how many steps. Thirty-one steps is the bathroom. Forty-four is exercise. If you go over sixty steps and down a staircase there's no other place they can be taking you. Every day. And they said 'Just one name and . . .' So I . . . And they wanted more names, so I . . . Every name I knew.

(*To* YANINA.) Your name.

YANINA (*fierce*). Whatever you had to do to live. I don't care. Whatever he had to do.

ALEXANDRA. Is . . . Where's Emiliano? Do you . . .

ALONSO *stands. He turns in a full circle, looking at all the* WOMEN *around him.*

ALONSO. I haven't seen him. I haven't seen anyone. Since the day they took us. They split us up and I haven't seen anyone since. They split us up and I haven't seen him since.

SOFIA *goes to him, takes his hand, kisses it, and sings very softly, a lullaby without words. When she's done she lets go his hand and turns away.*

SOFIA. Yani. Alonso's tired. Feed him. Put him to bed.

SOFIA goes into the house. We see the empty chair illuminated. She goes to it. On the other side of the stage the NARRATOR watches her.

YANINA *(to all the women)*. Whatever he had to do.

SOFIA returns with EMILIANO's chair.

ALEXANDRA. That's Emiliano's chair. Where are you going with my husband's chair?

SOFIA. To the river.

ALEXANDRA. Why?

SOFIA. You know why.

Poor Alexandra. So good and strong.

They send me back my men. The first two by the river, the third by the road. All dead. Now I go back to the river. To wait for the last.

Scene 25

The NARRATOR watches the women disappear. He is alone on the stage, for the first time without the chair.

NARRATOR. These are my last words.

Because if I stay, if I continue to speak, I will inevitably start to speak about myself.

So I am going.

Where am I going? Again: does it matter? Is it important?

Maybe I am disappearing into the story. Or maybe I am return-ing home under a false name, crossing the frontier, hoping I won't be recognized, entering the room where my children are trying to sleep, the son who looks just like me, the daughter born after I went into exile and whom I have never touched.

But you see: already I am talking about myself.

This is not my story.

I do not want to be the one figure in this story other people can identify with, find familiar, like a journalist who comes in, comfortably determines who is good and who is evil and then, feeling superior, tells the outside world about the atrocities.

I do not want to become that figure. It cannot be that the only way to make people care about this perverse fairy tale is to give them a personal hook.

What is known about me is already too much, more than enough: that this was how I brought myself back to life, my words going where my body could not go, my eyes witnessing what people back home did not dare to whisper and what people out here did not care about.

The world is full of stories about people with broken marriages, children who grow up without their father, men who dream of women who are true, journalists who explore and explain the mysteries of a world they do not belong to.

This is not about me.

This is not my story.

The NARRATOR *leaves – preferably going into the audience and out the theatre door.*

Scene 26

SOFIA *at the river with the chair.* TERESA *enters, dragging a chair behind her.*

SOFIA. What are you doing here?

TERESA. I came to wait too.

SOFIA. Whose chair?

TERESA. My brother's.

SOFIA. Sebastian?

TERESA. No. Fernando.

SOFIA. It's bitter tonight. You'll catch cold.

TERESA. I'm just as tough as you.

SOFIA. Start a fire. We're both old.

TERESA. There's no wood.

They look at the chairs. TERESA *sets hers on fire. Then* SOFIA *does.*

TERESA. Good fire. It makes me angry.

SOFIA. Two chairs. It's not much heat.

TERESA. Not yet. There'll be others.

Scene 27

EMMANUEL *at the Kastorias. We see two huge leather armchairs, facing upstage, cigar smoke curling up from them; they're both occupied but we can't see their occupants at first:* PHILIP KASTORIA *and his* BROTHER. *We will see Philip where indicated but we never see the brother. The brother speaks with a flat, slightly mechanical, very gravelly voice.* EMMANUEL *stands diffidently by.* BEATRICE KASTORIA *stands off to one side, staring out a window.*

PHILIP KASTORIA. Tell your captain I am not reassured.

EMMANUEL. Yes, Mr. Kastoria.

PHILIP KASTORIA. Two bodies, and now this multitude of widows.

I mean how much longer is this going to go on?

And this business of letting politicals go. I mean what is that? Whose idea of restoring order is that?

You're sure we can't get you something to drink, Emmanuel?

EMMANUEL. No, thank you very much, Mr. Kastoria.

BEATRICE KASTORIA. Are they feeding you, Emmanuel? You look thin.

PHILIP KASTORIA. Boy's always been thin, Beatrice.

BEATRICE KASTORIA. I've never forgiven Mr. Kastoria for giving you over to the army.

EMMANUEL. Thank you, Mrs. Kastoria.

BEATRICE KASTORIA. The people we have now are strange to us. I don't like them. Why don't you come back?

PHILIP KASTORIA. He's useful to me. The others are dribbling idiots.

EMMANUEL. Thank you, Mr. Kastoria.

PHILIP KASTORIA (*standing up, moving from chair*). I think your Captain is making a royal mess of this. My brother agrees.

Gestures to the chair.

I'd like you to tell your Captain that.

EMMANUEL. I think, Mr. Kastoria, that he's only trying to . . .

KASTORIA'S BROTHER. Lax.

EMMANUEL (*didn't catch it*). Excuse me, please, I'm sorry
but I . . .

KASTORIA'S BROTHER. Philip, tell him to tell his Captain that
he's being lax. Eight years of hard work will come undone
overnight, before you know it they'll be climbing the fence, like
before, digging their twisted fingers into our land again. Kill a
few more if they haven't learned the lesson yet. God help us
when the lower echelon military starts to think. Squeamish?
Replace him. Demote him. Give his job to this boy here.
Someone who'll cut it dead. This has been going on for weeks.
End it. Tell him that, Philip.

PHILIP KASTORIA. Yes, well . . .

KASTORIA'S BROTHER. What, the foreign press? Buried on
page fifty of the afternoon edition. They don't want to read this
garbage. They want to read about a little American girl trapped
in a well. In . . . *Texas!*

He laughs, enjoying saying 'Texas'.

Texas!

BEATRICE KASTORIA. I admire the Captain.

KASTORIA'S BROTHER. Philip, she's starting again . . .

BEATRICE KASTORIA. What do they want, these women? The
bodies of their husbands?

PHILIP KASTORIA. Beatrice, please.

BEATRICE KASTORIA. Well give them what they ask for, it's
the Christian thing.

PHILIP KASTORIA. Mrs. Kastoria has been nervous, Emmanuel,
she . . .

BEATRICE KASTORIA. Why do you always say I'm nervous
when I disagree with you? I'm not nervous. I'm afraid.

You know what I overheard the cooks in the kitchen saying,
Emmanuel?

PHILIP KASTORIA. Oh not this . . .

BEATRICE KASTORIA. They were talking about the women at
the river, and they were saying that they'd heard that bodies
were turning up everywhere, even here, even on our property,
in the private fields, in the orchards.

PHILIP KASTORIA (*making a ghost sound*). Oooooooooo . . .

BEATRICE KASTORIA. Shut up, Philip.

They were whispering but I could hear them. They said . . . that these corpses, they were decomposing and faceless. . .

PHILIP KASTORIA. Beatrice, please, that's very unpleasant.

BEATRICE KASTORIA. . . . and at night . . . they said they'd seen them walking around, dirty, and nothing could stop them because nothing can stop the dead.

KASTORIA'S BROTHER *laughs.*

BEATRICE KASTORIA. That's what she said, 'Nothing can stop the dead.'

And two nights ago, Philip I didn't tell you this but I woke up from a bad dream and I went downstairs and . . . and they'd left all the doors and windows open. The servants. Had left everything open. So that the dead could come in.

PHILIP KASTORIA (*going to her*). Bea, Bea . . .

You see, Emmanuel, why women wouldn't make good soldiers.

This is why this situation has to come to an end. It's gotten to be intolerable. I want you to tell your commanding officer that.

EMMANUEL. I will sir.

PHILIP KASTORIA. Or I'll have to use my own men. Understand?

EMMANUEL. Yes sir. I understand. I'll make sure the Captain understands.

The LIEUTENANT *enters.*

LIEUTENANT. Oh I think the captain is starting to understand all sorts of things, Emmanuel.

KASTORIA'S BROTHER. Ah, our saviour. I was on the phone to your father this morning.

In the background we see the other WOMEN *join* SOFIA *and the* FIRST WOMAN *at the riverbank. They carry wooden chairs.*

BEATRICE KASTORIA. Look, Philip, in the valley. Smoke.

LIEUTENANT. Yes, the women. All thirty-six widows. Building a bonfire.

Actually one isn't there. She drowned herself this morning.

(*To* EMMANUEL.) I think it was someone you know.

EMMANUEL *spins around to face the* LIEUTENANT. *They stare at each other.*

PHILIP KASTORIA (*looking at the smoke*). What in hell is going on?

LIEUTENANT. The whole village. Burning chairs.

KASTORIA'S BROTHER. Once they get their hands on fire . . .

PHILIP KASTORIA. That does it. I'm taking this into my own hands.

LIEUTENANT. That won't be necessary. I know this Captain.

All he needed was time.

Scene 28

The CAPTAIN *and the* LIEUTENANT *in the* CAPTAIN's *office.*

LIEUTENANT. It's an impressive blaze. It can be seen for miles. Everyone who sees it will wonder: who is in command in Camacho?

Little pause.

CAPTAIN. What do they want? I gave them back a. . . I showed them. How to get some of their men back, but they. . . it's like they're in love with death, begging me to pull the trigger.

LIEUTENANT. They want all their men back. Not just one. Not just some. All.

CAPTAIN. All? That's impossible.

LIEUTENANT. Impossible.

No more.

CAPTAIN. What?

LIEUTENANT. No more. That's all they'll say.

CAPTAIN. No more what?

LIEUTENANT. Ask them.

No more.

CAPTAIN. You must be very pleased.

LIEUTENANT. Pleased?

CAPTAIN. Well, you were right.

Now you'll get what you want. My resignation. And targets. Maybe hundreds. Vindication, recreation.

LIEUTENANT. Recreation? Captain, that's unfair.

> You think I enjoy this? That boy the other day? You think I enjoyed that?

CAPTAIN. Did you?

LIEUTENANT. I have a brother his age.

> You've tried to make things better for them, and predictably they'll have to suffer for your good intentions.

> They get the butt-end of everything, these people. I pity them.

CAPTAIN. And you despise me.

LIEUTENANT. Captain. We are wearing the same uniform.

CAPTAIN. Meaning you are ready to step into my boots.

LIEUTENANT. Meaning we share the same mother. Meaning that, like brothers, we stand by each other when mistakes are made.

Little pause.

I am yours to command.

Little pause.

CAPTAIN. Perhaps. . . perhaps I have. . . misjudged you.

Little pause.

Arrest the old Fuentes woman.

LIEUTENANT. I suggest a more direct approach.

CAPTAIN. Arrest her. The leader. More surgical.

LIEUTENANT. Just remember: Fires spread. There are lots of empty chairs, all over this valley, all over this country, ready for kindling. A lot of people are watching.

CAPTAIN. Watching me.

LIEUTENANT. Watching us.

CAPTAIN. Thank you.

> Perhaps, at some point in the future, you and I can spend a social evening together. In the city. Find some attractive women. The women around here are remarkably ugly.

LIEUTENANT. And remarkably stubborn.

They laugh.

LIEUTENANT. Finally, there's no reasoning with them. That crazy old woman.

CAPTAIN. Oh, I'll reason with her. I will show her how irresistibly persuasive reason can be. I'll break her fucking back.

LIEUTENANT. I'll go and get her.

CAPTAIN. And pick up her grandson while you're at it.

Little pause.

If you'd rather not do the boy I can send Emmanuel.

LIEUTENANT. That's – considerate of you, Captain.

CAPTAIN. It's nothing.

I had a special mother.

She taught me, as a child, to always be my brother's keeper.

LIEUTENANT. So did mine.

Scene 29

The FUENTES*'s house. The yard is strewn with the family's belongings.* FIDELIA *sits in the rubble.* ALONSO *sits on the steps of the house, holding the baby.*

YANINA *stands looking at the ruination. She goes to* ALONSO, *holds his head, pats him tenderly then gently takes the baby from his arms.* ALONSO *begins to cry quietly.* YANINA *walks the baby to the middle of the yard.*

ALEXANDRA *enters, breathing very hard, her hair wild, her clothes torn and her face bloody.*

ALEXANDRA. I'll never see him again.

YANINA. Don't say that.

He's too smart for them, he . . .

Fidelia?

FIDELIA *doesn't move.*

ALEXANDRA. Fidelia, Yani's talking to you.

YANINA. Take your uncle inside, Fidelia. He needs . . . to go inside.

FIDELIA *gets up. She and* ALEXANDRA *look at each other. Then* FIDELIA *takes* ALONSO *by the hand and leads him in.*

YANINA. You're a mess.

ALEXANDRA. Is the baby alright?

YANINA. Smiling.

You'll get him back. We'll co-operate. They'll bring him back, they wouldn't hurt a boy.

ALONSO *comes in.*

ALONSO. Yanina . . . ?

YANINA (*a beat, she goes to him, then says to* ALEXANDRA). All night he thrashes and he cries. His beautiful back is just scars.

Who are the men who did this to you, who do you see in your dreams? When will they pay for your scarring? I want to go into your dreams and drag those men out from the dark into daylight. I feel such . . . Rage. I think it will kill me.

FIDELIA *enters.*

ALEXANDRA. When they took Emiliano away I thought if I keep quiet and still they won't hurt him and he'll come back, someday, safe. They made me dance their steps every day ever since. Quiet and still, we all thought that, but there's always someone else they can take. I want my boy safe, but . . . We have to say an end to this. Finally, finally an end. They have to give us what's ours, living, dead, give us the men back, and if the men are murdered then give us their murderers. It's justice.

YANINA. Alonso. I'm going down to be with the women at the river.

ALONSO. Yani . . .

YANINA. If there was time, I could heal this. But there's no time now.

(*To* FIDELIA.) Take the baby.

YANINA *goes to* FIDELIA, *who backs away a step.* YANINA *hands her the baby, and then picks up a chair lying in the yard and begins to exit.*

FIDELIA. Mama . . . ?

ALEXANDRA. I'm going too.

FIDELIA. I want to go with you.

ALEXANDRA. Someone has to watch the baby.

FIDELIA. Alonso can do that.

ALEXANDRA. No. I don't think Alonso can.

FIDELIA. It's not my baby. I don't know what to do with him. If he gets upset . . .

ALEXANDRA. Feed him.

FIDELIA. If there's no food?

ALEXANDRA. Talk to him. Tell him stories.

FIDELIA. Mama, please don't go.

ALEXANDRA. Carry me with you, be a home for me.

She picks up the remaining chair.

I am your mother.

ALEXANDRA and YANINA put their arms around each other and go out of the yard to the river. FIDELIA watches them leave.

Scene 30

In a cell. The CAPTAIN, EMMANUEL and SOFIA. It's almost completely dark. There is a sound of water, dripping.

CAPTAIN. Talk. Talk, you old savage.

You think this is heroic? You think anyone even knows this is happening? I will load your body and their bodies onto the back of a wagon and dump you in a deep pit somewhere and after the quicklime and the dirt that's all, that's it, that's all that it will be. Just nothing. End it. You can. End it or I'll end it.

(*To* EMMANUEL). Lights, goddamit, do you think I'm a fucking bat?

EMMANUEL *turns on the lights. Everyone blinks.*

CAPTAIN. Bring in the boy.

SOFIA *reacts.*

CAPTAIN. Aha. She moves.

EMMANUEL *brings in ALEXIS. His hands are tied behind him, he has a stained canvas hood over his head, his shirt is ripped and one shoulder is bloody and obviously dislocated.*

SOFIA. He's a boy.

CAPTAIN. He's a man. This is as big as he gets.

The CAPTAIN *clamps his hand on* ALEXIS' *torn shoulder.* ALEXIS *almost screams.*

SOFIA. He can't help you.

CAPTAIN. But he's already got you talking. He's almost a miracle, this boy.

Pause.

Send the women to their homes. Co-operate or he'll go off into the darkest corner of the most godforsaken hell-hole prison, sure as there's a God in heaven he will, and then. . . .

You hear me? You will never see this – boy again. You hear me?

We will hurt him.

ALEXIS. Grandma . . . ?

SOFIA. Captain, do you have children, Captain?

A favour, in the name of your children.

I need a few minutes with him alone.

To say good-bye.

Pause.

CAPTAIN. Mother of God . . .

You're insane, this boy's alive and you can keep him alive, feel, feel . . .

He grabs her hand, forces it to ALEXIS' *chest, over his heart.*

CAPTAIN. He's alive. Feel his heart?

She keeps her hand on his heart. Pause. The CAPTAIN *slaps her hand away.*

CAPTAIN. What do I have to do to get you to go to the river?

SOFIA. We want the men to come home. All of them. You took them living we want them back living. If they're dead, we want to bury them.

CAPTAIN. But I offered you that, I . . .

SOFIA. And after that we want the killers punished. This is what we all want. All of us. By the river.

Little pause.

CAPTAIN. The tragedy of this country is . . . that it doesn't have to be dry and barren, it's waiting to blossom, it wants to be green but . . . no one understands that you move forward in steps, not all at once, and if you ask too much you wind up with nothing but dust. This boy . . . could learn to read. He could vote, he could become . . . something good for his country, he could do that, a citizen.

His pain, his ugly death . . . is your dream for him, not mine.

The CAPTAIN *unholsters his gun, hold it near* ALEXIS' *head.*

CAPTAIN. Ask her to save your life. Ask her. ASK HER!

He rips off the hood. ALEXIS *closes his eyes, stands swaying.*

ALEXIS. Grandma.

Silence.

SOFIA. A few minutes.

Pause.

CAPTAIN. What do I get if I give you that?

SOFIA. Maybe some peace. You'll need it. Later.

Peace.

CAPTAIN. I'm not granting any more requests. You have nothing to say to him anyway.

He cocks the trigger.

SOFIA. Could I touch him?

CAPTAIN. What for?

SOFIA. Please.

Little pause.

CAPTAIN. You tire me, woman.

Indicates with his head that she can touch ALEXIS. SOFIA *approaches her grandson, touches his heart again. There is a moment where nothing happens, and then the lights change suddenly.* SOPHIA *and* ALEXIS *are alone.*

SOFIA. Can you hear me?

ALEXIS. Yes.

SOFIA. They can't hear us, my little man.

I can't protect you, my baby. Do you understand why?

ALEXIS. No.

SOFIA. Do you forgive me?

Little pause.

ALEXIS. Yes.

SOFIA. I have something to tell you.

There are villages of the living and villages of the dead, surrounding us always.

Press up against the wall. Behind you. There's a hand in the stone. Reach for it, hold it.

ALEXIS. I'm scared, I . . .

SOFIA. Yes yes, the hand is there. Do you feel it?

ALEXIS. I don't feel anything.

SOFIA. It's your father. You know his hand.

ALEXIS. Yes.

SOFIA. It's a strong hand. It's so gentle for you. So you can be brave. For the one who comes after you, for the ones who come after. People like us don't die.

We will be there in the stones of the wall, you and I and the many others, we will be there together, my little man, my baby, till the walls come down.

The lights return, the CAPTAIN *takes her hand from the boy's chest. He looks at* SOFIA.

CAPTAIN. God forgive you. God forgive us all.

A blackout. First one gunshot, then another. Lights up immediately. FIDELIA *and the* BABY. *Below them, at the river, the* WOMEN *and the* SOLDIERS *gather.*

Scene 31

FIDELIA (*to the baby*). You must learn how to talk. You'll need to talk. There are things you'll have to tell.

But if you decide never to speak, your stories will get told anyway. There are stories that cry out to be told and if the words aren't there they will seep through the skin.

The wind carries them, the smoke does, the river does, the words of the story will find their way, from the farthest, loneliest places, to places where there are people willing to hear . . .

I can wait. I can wait for you to speak. I'm patient. I can wait a long time.

She exits.

Brilliant sunlight by the river. The WOMEN; *opposite them, many* SOLDIERS, *heavily armed. The* CAPTAIN *and* EMMANUEL, *waiting. The* LIEUTENANT *arrives.*

CAPTAIN. This country's hopeless. They'll have to depopulate it, the whole country and bring in other people, people from outside, people with some other kind of mind.

Pause. The CAPTAIN *looks at the* WOMEN.

LIEUTENANT. Perhaps you'd rather I gave the order, sir?

CAPTAIN. I can do that.

The SOLDIERS *draw their rifle bolts, assume positions.*

Women: this is your last chance. Go to your homes. Obey, or I will signal my men to move you. They will use as much force as is necessary.

Little pause.

Men: I want the riverbank cleared.

The CAPTAIN *looks again at the* WOMEN; *they look at him. There is suddenly the loud cry of an animal, a blackbird or . . . Everyone, the* WOMEN, *the* SOLDIERS, *looks up. Then back down, because the river is beginning to sound again. The* WOMEN *move to the river, silently, then go into the water and carry a body out onto the riverbank. They advance towards the soldiers, then stop. They look at each other. Then they advance again – perhaps dancing, perhaps singing, perhaps only moving forward, as they rock the body like a newborn child. Blackout.*

End of play.

Acknowledgements in the Guise of an Afterword

The origins of this play go back twenty years.

It was 1976, and for the last three years, ever since General Augusto Pinochet had seized power in Chile, I had wandered over Latin America and Europe, finally settling down in Holland. It was there, in Amsterdam, that the story which remains at the core of *Widows* first came to me.

I was working on a painful series of poems about the missing, men and women who, snatched from their homes by the secret police in the silence of the night, are never heard of again, their bodies denied to their relatives as if they had never existed. As I wrote, I could feel myself being turned into a bridge through which the living and the dead were trying to communicate, a burial mound where they could meet and mourn and touch. By allowing the voices of the disappeared and the families waiting for their return to speak to each other using my faraway words I was also finding a way of going back myself to the faraway country where my own body and, of course, these very words I was writing, were forbidden, placing myself imaginatively in that place I had escaped, that story I could not share except as a witness, except as a channel for those voices which seemed to be taking possession of my throat.

One night – it was early, just after dinner – I was visited by an image, almost a hallucination: an old woman by a river, holding the hand of a body that had just washed up on its shores. And the certainty that this scene had happened before, that this was not the first time that that river had yielded a dead man to the arms of that old and twisted woman.

I wrote all night, the same poem over and over again, trying to hear that woman I had invented and who nevertheless seemed to have a life of her own, I spent those long dark European hours trying to drag that woman out of the darkness inside me, the darkness on the other side of the world where she lay trapped in oblivion and indifference, I sat there and tried to understand word for word what she was saying and that so few in the alien world I unwillingly lived in seemed to care about. And by dawn, a new poem, almost like a new born child, was there on the table where we ate our meals and where I also wrote my work back then in exile, that poem which gave origin to *Widows* was waiting for my wife Angelica, always my first reader, to give her opinion.

This was the poem:

What did you say – they found another one?
– I can't hear you – this morning
another one floating
in the river?
talk louder – so you didn't even dare
no one can identify him?
the police said not even his mother
                    not even the mother who bore him
                    not even she could
they said that?
the other women already tried – I can't understand
                                what you're saying,
they turned him over and looked at his face, his hands
                                they looked at,
            right,
they're all waiting together,
silent, in mourning,
on the riverbank,
they took him out of the water
he's naked
        as the day he was born,
there's a police captain
and they won't leave until I get there?
He doesn't belong to anybody,
you say he doesn't belong to anybody?

        tell them I'm getting dressed,
            I'm leaving now

        if the captain's the same one as
            last time
        he knows
            what will happen.
            that body will have my name
            my son's my husband's
                    my father's
            name
I'll sign the papers tell them
        tell them I'm on my way,
            wait for me
and don't let that captain touch him
don't let that captain take one step closer
            to him.

Tell them not to worry:
I can bury my own dead.

So. It was done. The old woman had a presence, she had been given a voice, she was free to roam the earth in that poem and speak her lines. I had done my job. Now it was up to her to do hers.

Except that the old woman was not content with this. In the fictitious universe of poetry she had defied that captain and now she would not leave me alone in my own unfortunately quite existent historical universe of exile.

As the years went by, I could not rid myself of the certainty that there was more, much more, to her story than what I had written, that in the poem I had merely grazed the outer skin of that pain, of that fierce determination of hers not to let that captain bury her dead, and that she wanted me to go deeper, she wanted the world to know what happened before, what happened afterwards, she wanted – in brief – to be narrated, told in time, filled with a world and filling it. That old woman wanted a further destiny and she would not rest until I had given it to her.

Perhaps she would never have been successful – after all, I cannot dispense that sort of service to every one of the crazed literary creatures who mill around inside me and clamour for the light of day and paper – if she had not formed an alliance with another obsession of mine that was just as difficult to get rid of: the need to be published in my country, to reach the audience that the dictatorship was denying me. I was particularly worried about the young people back in Chile – and in other countries of Latin America, Argentina, Uruguay, Brazil, so many of them suffering the same tyranny, the same armies imposing death and defeat. And I began to wonder oh so slowly if I could not write a novel dealing with the disappeared, telling the story of that old woman and that river and those bodies and that captain, but using a pseudonym, disguising my name and perhaps even, yes, disguising the country where this was happening. A great deal of the horror of Chile was, after all, enhanced by the fact that this sort of tragedy and this sort of resistance had occurred before in history, that we seemed to be repeating, forty years after the Nazi experiments, some of the same endless sorrows and iniquities. What if I were to make up a Danish author who, living under the German occupation of his country, had written this story, a fictitious author who would himself be, I decided, a missing person? What if that story about an old woman by a river in a place like, say, Greece, had been lost all these years and only recently located and now was being published for the first time? What if that novel, supposedly written by that Danish author, happened to be translated into Spanish and sold in Chile? Could the authorities of my country object? How would they know that I was the real author?

Some time in the summer of 1978, I began to write that novel which I called, from the very beginning, *Widows*. I could not have written of such loss if I had not, at that time, been accompanied by my wife, who was pregnant with the boy who was to be our son Joaquin, if I had not lifted my eyes from the page that was taking me into the hell of those women on a river bank and seen our eldest son Rodrigo playing cheerfully nearby. The joy that I was experiencing was precisely what was being stolen from my protagonists.

And as, in the months that followed, I answered the call of that old woman and gave her a world in which to live, I embarked as well on a different sort of operation, of a less literary kind: I appealed to those who, in the real world of real frontiers and real censors, could help me fool the dictatorship in Chile. My primary partners in this wild scam turned out to be two fellow writers both of whom are no longer living – and whose affection and loyalty I can now acknowledge. My friend Heinrich Böll, the German Nobel Prize winner, who had already helped Solzhenitzin smuggle his manuscripts out of the repressive Soviet Union, was delighted with the opportunity of assisting a Chilean writer do the reverse and smuggle his manuscript into a country where he could not be published. He would preface the book, Böll said with a twinkle, as we set drinking tea in his house near Cologne: he would explain to the readers that the son of an unknown Danish author had come to him with his father's long lost novel that the world should now read forty years after its creator's death at the hands of the Nazi secret police. And a month later in Paris the Argentine writer Julio Cortázar who had been like a brother to me in those years of exile, told me that he would gladly and mischievously appear as the 'translator' of the book into Spanish from the French – though of course the text that would be seeing the light of day would be my own original Spanish-language version.

All I needed now was for a publisher, who brought out books in Chile, Argentina and Spain and had originally shown some enthusiasm for the project when I had mentioned it to him, to give me the green light. But when the man read the manuscript, he demurred. He wasn't ready, he told me, to risk his whole enterprise on this sort of adventure: the military would quickly see through the ruse and then I would be safely out of harm's way, still banished, but he and his employees and his investors would have to suffer Pinochet's displeasure. There is nothing an army hates more than being made fun of.

So I was left stranded with my old woman on this side of the barrier of fear that still surrounded Chile. She had been unable to surreptitiously infiltrate me back into my country. But, she suggested, the world was still there, as much in need of this story as my country. We should circulate it abroad, wherever we could until that remote day when Chile would be free to receive my words and hers.

I proceeded to publish the novel under my own name. It was no longer necessary to bother Böll and Cortázar. Several foreign editors suggested that I should now make the story more overtly Latin American and militant and denunciatory. Instead, I decided to preserve the framing device of the Danish author and to keep the Greek setting for the story. I did not want readers to feel that this was merely some exotic abuse in lands that they had barely heard of. I wanted them to ask themselves about the connections between my country and theirs, my present and their past, our present and their future. And besides, I had discovered that the distancing of my urgent reality back home, my ability to pretend someone else had written that narrative, had had a liberating effect on it. This allegorical approach helped to solve an artistic dilemma that besieges many authors who deal with contemporary political issues: how to write about matters that have extraordinary documentary weight without being subjected to the grinding jaws of a 'realism' that is often unable to depict the complexity of what is truly happening? To give just one example: when I wrote that novel, no bodies of the missing had yet been unearthed, neither in Chile nor elsewhere. If I had written only about what was effectively transpiring in my land, I would have been limited to tracing and copying what history had already materialised. Instead, I imagined a different scenario, one that history was hiding at the moment but which would, in the years to come, reveal itself: I prophesied that the bodies would begin to appear, that nobody could stop the dead from coming home, that the women were bringing them back against silence and oppression and, in effect, as time went by, they began to emerge from the rivers and the mine shafts and the fields and the sands of Chile and Latin America, they came as if from the depths of the imagination of the world. I didn't want to be trapped into reproducing what existed out there. I wanted my literature to explore an alternative future that my imagination could see and that perhaps could some day emerge from reality itself. I also saw my story going beyond mere denunciations of the terrors of a dictatorship, asking questions about memory and gender and betrayal and community and writing itself which should not be subsumed in what seemed to be the political questions the text posed.

This dilemma of how to tell a story that was historical in as much as it derived from the suffering of real human beings, but that simultaneously had to obey aesthetic and literary laws of representation that demanded freedom from that immediate history, would come back to haunt me in the story's next embodiment, when many years later, one day in 1985, I got a call from Judy James, then with the Mark Taper Forum in Los Angeles, who had been given the novel by my friend Deena Metzger and who thought it cried out to be a play and, eventually she thought, a film.

The old woman inside me agreed. She wanted more people to see her life, to witness how she had not allowed death to dictate that life. She wanted to live again, this time on stage.

Thus began one of the longest and most arduous creative odysseys of my existence. The poem had taken a night to compose and the novel, a year. The play was to bedevil me for almost a decade.

Widows the play had many incarnations. Under the diligent guiding light of my director at the Taper, Bob Egan, and supported with verve by Gordon Davidson, the artistic director of the company, my play went through many rewrites and two major workshops where the actors gave everything of themselves and, in return, showed me no mercy with their questions. I felt that I knew the women of this play, knew who they were, from what despair and loss and ambiguity they acted: it was the men, the military, who ended up being a real enigma, and in those workshops Richard Jordan and René Auberjenois, who incarnated the Captain, and Tony Plana, who played the Lieutenant, were particularly helpful. But advice was not enough: I needed to see it fully staged to try and figure out what was wrong. In 1988, Diane and Johnny Simons of the Hip Pocket Theatre in Fort Worth, Texas, premiered a version that had just won a New American Plays Award at the Kennedy Center; and that same summer I went on to get another production starring Tony Musante and directed by Kay Matschullat at the Williamstown Theatre Festival. Reviews and audiences were enthusiastic, but I knew, as I watched the staging, that the play had not yet freed itself from the magic of the novel.

After yet another rewrite and another disappointing reading at the always faithful Taper, Bob Egan and Gordon Davidson proposed in 1989 a different solution: perhaps I needed someone else to come in and collaborate with me.

I was sceptical, but the old woman inside me kept nagging, the dead and the missing inside us would not leave either of us alone. So I reluctantly agreed to read some of the plays of the man my friends at the Taper thought could help me bring my vision to fruition. He was a relatively unknown playwright but was bound, they were sure, for great things.

His name was Tony Kushner.

When I read his plays, *A Bright Room Called Day*, and the first draft of an absolutely compelling drama entitled *Angels in America*, I agreed that he was indeed the right person to work with me. Tony's vision might be different from mine, but he was struggling with my same demons of expression, confronting ways in which politics and imagination intersect, how to depict suffering and repression without sinking into hopelessness, how to be colloquial and simultaneously mythical, how to show human resistance and resilience without being propagandistic or doctrinaire, how to recognise that we have the enemy inside and the best people are capable of the most terrible things.

If I deluded myself into believing that I was the bridge the missing had been looking for to enter the world and speak to it, Tony became in effect the bridge I had been looking for to enter the world of theatre and reach the U.S. audience which I had found trouble in connecting to this particular story so removed politically and aesthetically from the typical American tradition. For the next two years, interrupted by several trips of my own back to Chile where I could now go and where we were in the process of ousting Pinochet from power, Tony patiently helped me craft *Widows* into the play it had always promised to be, provided dialogue and characters and rhythm, day after day after day. He is the co-author of this text, its midwife, the hands that helped the play, like a child, to grow. I cannot thank him enough for what he taught me, for his loyalty to the old woman and her family, for his friendship to me and my own family.

And yet, the play which finally opened on the main stage of the Mark Taper Forum directed by Bob Egan in 1991 – ten days after another play of mine, *Death and the Maiden* had its premiere at the Royal Court in London – was still not exactly what I wanted. As I watched the performance in Los Angeles, there was something still missing, something the novel had possessed and that this play, for all its power, had not yet managed to achieve. I had no idea what that missing something could possibly be – only that I had now strayed too far from the original vision and that I had to find a way to get back to it, that the text still beckoned me to journey with it for one last time.

My next few years were filled with *Death and the Maiden* – and Tony's own stunning success with *Angels in America;* so neither he nor I found the time or the tranquillity to return to *Widows* again. And yet, for me, in the back of my mind, it was always there, demanding to find its voice and be complete. This secret dialogue with myself might well have gone on forever if the

Andrew Wylie Agency had not one day received a call from Ian
Brown at the Traverse Theatre: he wanted to do our play up in
Edinburgh. My answer to him – as it had been to others who had
recently inquired about possible new productions – was that it
needed one more rewrite before it would be ready. But my agent,
Deborah Karl, would not let me off the hook that easily. She
insisted that I should say yes to the Traverse's offer and force
myself once and for all to finish the play. And she was right: when
I concentrated on the characters and structure again, I discovered
the changes I thought the play required. However, when I met
my co-author for lunch in New York and told him what I wanted
to do, Tony said, with his usual generosity, that I should go ahead
without him, that I had to run this last lap to the finish line on
my own.

And that was how I found myself again writing alone, wrestling
with my solitude and that old woman's affliction, offering *Widows*
one last ritual elaboration, one more labour of love. Besides a
couple of minor alterations, shifts in emphasis, a heightening of the
lyrical and mythical qualities of the drama, the major modification
– one which, in fact, I only could have accomplished by myself, by
going into my own pain one last time – was to frame the play with
a narrator who is himself, as I had been, an exile who watches,
witnesses, suffers the action from afar. I suspect that my decision
to introduce this enigmatic male figure into the action and then let
him be swallowed by it, will be controversial, and I do not intend
in this afterword to defend his presence. Suffice it to say that I felt,
as I wrote him, and continue to feel now, that this particular story
cannot be told without that intermediary between the real audience
and the mythical characters. I needed someone like him to distance
that tragedy while paradoxically bringing it closer to us and our
impure contemporary world. The exile that had been at the origin
of my relationship with that old woman and her missing loved
ones had to be infiltrated back into the story. Perhaps in its next
incarnation – in *Widows* the film, which I am sure will eventually
find its way into a world in dire need of its message – that narrator
will again disappear, this time fused into the tender and alien lens
of the camera.

Even so, having finished that version, it still took Ian Brown and
the friends at the Traverse several years to find the funds to stage a
play that needed so many actors and that dealt with issues that are
so dark and unyielding and apparently remote.

It should be clear by now that this play has arrived at its final
published version only because it was supported through two
decades by countless men and women who believed in it. Some

of those names have been alluded to in these pages. Space does not allow so many deserving others to receive my gratitude here, but they do know who they are. Thanks to you, one and all, for having helped to bring this story to life.

I have left for the end the most important acknowledgment and recognition of all.

I made up that old woman.

I invented her and her family and that river and that captain who does not know how to deal with her.

If she could come from my imagination, however, it was because she had been placed there, sparked into being, inspired into existence by real women who searched for real bodies in a real world more cruel and inhuman than anything I finally described in my fiction.

Democracy has returned now to Chile and to so many other countries where those widows resisted the military and demanded their men back. Democracy has returned, but many of those women are still waiting for the return of their fathers, their husbands, their brothers, their sons, many of them are still waiting for a river or a god to bring those bodies back from the dead. And the bodies are also waiting, somewhere, are still accusing the men who murdered them, are still waiting for justice to be done, are still demanding to be remembered by a society that is all too willing to forget.

It is to those waiting women, the women who are the hidden and silent storytellers of this tale that came to me as if in a dream twenty years ago, it is to them that *Widows* is finally dedicated.

Ariel Dorfman, December 1996

A Nick Hern Book

Widows first published in Great Britain in 1997
by Nick Hern Books Limited, 14 Larden Road, London W3 7ST,
in association with the Traverse Theatre, Edinburgh

Widows copyright © 1997 by Ariel Dorfman

Afterword copyright © 1997 by Ariel Dorfman

Front cover picture: Euan Myles

Typeset by Country Setting, Woodchurch, Kent TN26 3TB

Printed by Cox and Wyman, Reading, Berks

ISBN 1-85459-376-5

A CIP catalogue record for this book is available from
the British Library